Work from Home: Starting & Running a Profitable Freight Broker Business

A comprehensive step-by-step Startup guide for the 21st Century

By

Julia Albright

Cover & Book Design by Robin Wright

Contents

Introduction

Are you tired of working a regular job? Are you retired and looking for a way to own your business? Is being your own boss something you have always dreamed of? Whether you have thought about starting a home based business, or have legally established your company, this guide will teach you the ins and outs of starting a Freight Brokerage Firm.

You can begin right from your home with a laptop, time, dedication, and industry knowledge. I can help you with the later 2, the laptop and time are all on you!

I've been a serial entrepreneur for over 20 years, starting online businesses and helping thousands of people just like yourself start the next chapter of their lives.

For many people, working from home has been an extremely attractive option. However, many get stuck in the initial stages becoming stagnant in their planning and follow-through

This detailed book is designed to help you get your business up and running without spending hours upon hours doing research. I've done it all for you.

Now, I'm not saying that there won't be work to do on your part. There most certainly will be, but you should be able to save a lot of time and energy by simply following the suggestions and tips provided here.

When I was laid off from my job at the State of Ohio back in 2010, I sold Kirby Vacuum cleaners, and I worked for DialAmerica selling magazine subscriptions. I even sold Avon. It was one day, back in 2015, when I was trying to unbury my way through boxes of Skin So Soft® and costume jewelry to get to the kitchen that it hit me.

I looked around at not only those boxes, but basically everything in my house. If trucks are moving more freight, that means Americans are more productive and earning more money.

Take a look around your own home or your office. If you do a quick mental inventory, you too will realize what I did. That there isn't anything that we use on a daily basis, or for decoration, or display, that didn't get to us either partially or entirely by truck.

So I did what any red-blooded American with a Wi-Fi connection and a laptop would do. I set out to investigate and learn about this business as much as possible. I wanted to know how I could bring my folding chair to the Transportation & Freight Industry table, and this book is a compilation of all that research, data, and planning that I went through.

If you are asking yourself why I chose a freight brokering journey, there are quite a few reasons why. Starting your own home based brokerage firm is a lucrative, long-term strategy to own a business that ultimately helps fuel the economy.

According to the Bureau of Transportation Statistics 2017 Report (https://www.bts.gov/sites/bts.dot.gov/files/docs/FFF_2017.pdf) on Freight Facts and Figures, "The transportation sector is an integral part of the U.S. economy. It employs millions of people and comprises 8.9 percent of the Nation's economic activity as measured by gross domestic product (GDP)."

With a generally positive outlook for the U.S. economy, U.S. manufacturing is expected to rise faster than the general economy. The MAPI Foundation states (https://tinyurl.com/mapifoundation) increased capital growth and higher exports are going to boost the manufacturing industry. They also forecast production will increase by 3.9 percent in 2019, and will slow at a steady pace to 2.4 percent in 2020, then expected to drop to 1.9 percent in 2021.

There were significant changes in the freight brokerage industry in 2013. These changes came in the form of legislation, which forced some people out of the industry. This was due to stricter regulations, which then opened the doorway to new brokers.

These fresh faces had a brand new type of energy and a big picture outlook for the future. This allowed them to come in and make a lucrative profit in this business.

This changing of the guard leads to rejuvenation in the industry, with evolving and modernizing of standards, thanks to new and innovative technology.

Now is the absolute best time to be in the freight broker business. There are tons of great reasons to contemplate starting your own firm from home. There is an increasing demand for emerging new brokers who can meet the needs of an ever increasing and changing economy.

I've tried to keep this guide as simple and entertaining as possible, as you set about to learn the following topics.

Chapter I: What does a Freight Brokerage Firm Do?

In this first chapter, we'll examine what a freight brokerage firm does.

- Before you begin about starting the business, it's important for to you understand what is involved so you can decide right away if this is the right fit for you.

- Just as your goals and skill set will evolve in your new journey, so should your network. This is a general life lesson and even more important in the transportation and freight industry. Learn why you need to meet the key players in the industry and who they are.

- Education, experience, and training means the difference between success and failure as an entrepreneur. You need to understand not only the industry you want to start a business in, but also what entrepreneurship is all about, and what it takes to become an entrepreneur. You can manage your 9-5 and work on your dreams at the same time.

- Learn about the daily operations of a freight brokerage firm so you know what you can expect in a typical day's work. Look at what's required and identify the skills you already have. Skills you can simply strengthen, and then identify areas where you can improve and start to seek out those resources online. Google is your best friend now, aside from me, of course.

- Every new business needs software to automate, process, store information, and keep them in compliance with industry standards. We will show you all of the software, both free and paid, you will need to get started with your new freight brokerage business from home.

- As we wrap up Chapter I, we will walk you through the "Life of a Load" from start to finish and your role as the broker. You can see step-by-step how your freight brokerage firm can have an impact. You will start to form ideas on how you and your business can bridge gaps.

Chapter II: Federal Requirements for Freight Brokerage Firms

Chapter II is about compliance, which is the not so fun stuff of starting a business. It can be frustrating and sometimes hard to understand compliance, which often deters new innovators from seeing the idea through to its fruition.

I've broken down those boring terms and made them fun with links to resources and forms as much as possible. You will learn:

- Freight Broker Compliance Requirements

- Record Keeping and Accurate Accounting Requirements

- Misrepresenting Yourself as a Carrier

- Charging Carriers for Services

- Rules for Different Goods Shipped

- Food Safety Regulations and Laws

- Bond Renewal Laws

Chapter III: The Costs of Doing Business and the Time Required to Run a Home-based Freight Brokerage Firm

- You cannot make money without spending money. If you are looking for something to start without investing in yourself, then you can expect very little reward, and this venture is not for you. This is not only an investment of money but also your time. You have to be committed and stay the course to see the results you want.

- In order to run a successful freight brokerage firm, you need to establish relationships that matter — specifically, financial experts and advisors.

Chapter IV: The Working from Home Mindset for Freight Brokerage Firms

- Working from home requires a certain mindset, regardless of what industry or niche you choose. If you get nothing else from this book, take away the knowledge in this chapter on how to get laser focused and organized.

- You, Yourself and You: Working from home and more importantly, running a business from home, requires that you get used to spending time alone and undistracted. I'll teach you how to not want to staple your eyelids closed from loneliness and boredom.

- Even though you are starting a home based business, it's important that you remember you have to interact with others in order to grow your business. You will have to bring in new customers, clients, and eventually employees. In this section, I'll show you how to develop communication with your truckers.

- We will wrap up Chapter IV with tips on how to set up your home office for success and comfort. Your environment is a key to your mindset. In addition to that, being organized and having the right setup will ensure your long-term success.

Chapter V: Pricing Your Freight Brokerage Services

- Before you can market your services, you need to know how much you are going to charge. I'll share with you the typical price range of service fees across the country.

- Learn how to negotiate your truckload pricing with a few neat tricks.

- Competitor research will play a crucial role in how you determine pricing. Therefore, it is imperative that you do your research on your competitors both locally and globally. I'll show you not only what to look for and compare, but why it's important, and the best places to do your opposition research.

Chapter VI: Choosing a Niche and Marketing Your Brokerage Firm

Market research for your new business is critical to your initial start-up phase and will help determine your overall sustainability and growth. I will show you what to search for, where to search, and how to organize the data to start making decisions.

- One of the biggest myths I've ever heard is that some of the greatest salespeople are natural-born sellers. This is a common fallacy. Great sales reps, who do well, build teams and make money have a system that's repeatable and scalable to continue to bring in new business. You will learn how to pitch to your target audience without sounding like a car salesman, but actually providing customized value for each client.

- Once you have your perfect pitch, someone needs to hear it, right? I'll teach you where to find carriers and customers and the most trusted way to reach out and message them directly without violating spam laws.

- Now that you have learned how to pitch your services and how to price them, it's time you start looking for new clients and customers. I'll teach you how to market your freight business effectively, building your database of useful key players and industry professionals.

- Next, we'll focus on where to find these people. There are tons of hidden treasures on the internet for finding leads. I'll share my insider secrets and resources with you so you can get a leg up on the competition.

- Once you have your leads, we'll talk about how to deliver your pitch you created. Delivery, approach, and timing are key, as well as who you give or send your pitch to.

Chapter VII: Regulatory Agencies and Resources for Freight Brokerage Firms

This chapter is a glossary of links to regulatory agencies and contacts that will help you stay on top of the law and your regulatory responsibilities. They can also guide you on where to find forms and potentially connect you with carriers.

I will also include a depository or helpful online resources for your reference.

Chapter VIII: Diversity and Growth Tips for Freight Brokerage Firms

In this chapter, we'll examine how to grow and keep growing your new business. We will talk about change in the industry and how to obtain new customers why not remaining stagnant.

Chapter IX: A Final Word

I take a moment to share some last words of wisdom and impart some important advice that I have personally learned.

Chapter X: Glossary and FAQ for Freight Brokerage Firms

The final chapter of this guide is a glossary and FAQ of the entire freight broker industry. Use this as a reference when doing your own research. Start to familiarize yourself with these industry terms, so when you are having conversations with other industry professionals, you can speak intelligently and with confidence.

Chapter I: What Does a Freight Brokerage Firm Do?

In the simplest terms possible, a freight brokerage firm/freight broker is the essential key piece that links the shipping requirements and transportation carriers together. Each has its own agenda, timetable, and profit goals.

As a freight broker, it will be your business' mission to match up various cargo with the appropriate carriers (truckers). You act as either an individual or a corporation that simply matches the shippers with the correct transportation service providers to safely transport those goods and services.

It is then your role to do the research and legwork to find the distinguished, reputable, and most importantly, properly licensed carriers and shipping companies in the transportation industry. You can also work with transportation and logistics coordinators, which we will discuss in the upcoming section about industry players.

When a manufacturer wants to ship their product to market, they have to have a truck or carrier to do so. As a freight broker, you will work closely with the shipping companies and manufacturers to help them find the right transportation companies.

Utilizing research, analysis, and comparison, you will find the carriers that can help the manufacturer, your client, meet their order demands. The main goal is to save your client, the shipper, money by pairing them with the best option.

You do this by negotiating the prices between the shipper and the carrier, making adjustments that are in the best interest of getting the order fulfilled. In return, you receive a commission for your services.

WHAT IS A FREIGHT BROKER'S FUNCTION?

"Transportation intermediaries leverage their knowledge, investment in technology and people resources to help both the shipper and carrier succeed," - Robert A. Voltmann, President & CEO of the Transportation Intermediaries Association.

Brokers and brokerage firms are an integral and invaluable part of our economy. In some instances, companies even use their brokerage firm as a traffic division. This allows the brokerage firm to oversee their entire shipping manifesto, ensuring all the management and transportation needs are met.

There are two essential key functions in the freight broker business: you, the freight broker, and your carriers (the trucks). Without either, there is essentially no business. If you have a million loads, but not one single truck to transport them, you are dead in the water. Likewise, if you have a million trucks and nothing to ship, you make zero dollars and again dead in the water.

HISTORY OF FREIGHT BROKERING

There are no official historical records of the exact date of how freight brokering came into existence. Although, we do know that there is an official record of a lucrative brokerage business operating as early as the 1800s, with the birth of the first "backhaul."

A "backhaul" is a load or shipment that allows the industry's carriers a way of earning profit in an area they specifically service, or where they happen to have clients or accounts already. This occurs when a carrier was forced to return home empty-handed.

Your job as the freight broker, as well as one of the main goals of the carrier, will be the backhaul, or return-trip of a commercial truck that is functioning as your carrier network. Why do you want to focus on that? Let me explain in further detail.

UTILIZING THE BACKHAUL

When your carrier (trucking company) that you have chosen to partner with delivers all of their shipments, you want them to come back as quickly as possible so they can pick up another load.

There is nothing worse than having a customer call needing a shipment picked up and you don't have equipment or room to get it done for them. If they find a different company that can meet all of their needs, including last-minute demands, 9 times out of 10, they are going to go somewhere else for that shipment. They may not come back to you for future shipments. This means a lost opportunity for you, as the freight broker, and for the carrier.

Your carrier will occasionally call you and ask you to provide them with loads to pick up and bring back home, thus creating backhauls. This not only saves time but also saves money. When these situations occur, it is in the best interest of the freight broker to try and negotiate a lower transport fee per mile.

The average range is anywhere from 10-30%, which allows you to still earn a profit for the service you just fulfilled for your customer. This also preserves the revenue you just helped the carrier earn, even though it's a lower rate that you negotiated.

So why on earth would a carrier agree to take a lower transport fee on their rate? Who wouldn't want to return home with something in their truck and wallet rather than having both of them empty?

Every single second that a truck is not out on the road is lost revenue, and in some cases, can be an added expense for the business owner. Some of the most costly expenses include insurance, making their monthly payments on their truck or trailer, buying fuel for the trucks, and paying the driver.

Now, this is not to say that all carriers will be willing to accept a lower rate for a backhaul, but there are plenty of them that do. When partnering with a carrier, make one of the questions you ask, "Do you accept a discounted rate on backhauls?"

Pretty amazing, right? There's so much to learn, and the possibilities of how you run your business are literally endless.

So now that you know you need a solid carrier on your team, let's discuss the other key players in the industry and the importance of each one.

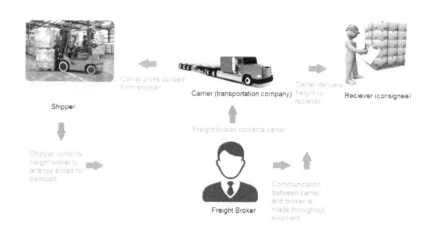

Players in the Freight Brokerage Industry

Have you ever heard of the saying, your net-worth is a direct reflection of your network? While you know it costs money to grow and start a business, an investment is 99% necessary in order to even get your doors open. But what is it that allows some to succeed while others fail?

It's one small overlooked factor; the people who succeed also invest in business relationships. *Your number one asset is your Rolodex.*

In this area of your human capital, I would suggest that you do not go fast, and you do not go cheap. Your business relationships are the lifeblood of your success.

With ever-advancing technology and methods we can use to contact our clients and customers, personal relationships in today's world boil down to not how much time we spend with each other, but how many interactions we have with each other. It's sad but true.

In an industry as wide and diverse as freight and transportation, it requires a workforce that is equally yoked. Now, please do not let these titles confuse you or misdirect your focus. Some of them are indeed quite similar, with maybe only a function separating them.

I've attempted to keep it as clear as possible on which key players you should be focused on while building and growing your home based freight brokerage firm.

Let's have a look at who these key industry players are and what they do.

KEY INDUSTRY ROLES DEFINED

"Freight Broker": This is your role as the CEO of your own home-based freight brokerage firm. You will be the person who connects the shippers to the appropriate carriers.

"Shipper": The "shipper" would be the individual or company who has physical products or goods that need to be transported from one place to another to be sold.

"Motor Carrier": A "motor carrier" is what is known in the industry as the trucking company or you might even hear it called "transportation." A private motor carrier transports its own cargo, usually as a part of a business that makes, consumes, profits or buys the cargo that is being hauled.

A private motor carrier will provide its own goods along with its own transportation. They are required by law to have a USDOT number, but they do not need operating authority.

"Freight Forwarder": A "freight forwarder," while often confused with the role of a freight broker, is not the same thing. Although many people interchange the two, they could not be more notably different. "Freight forwarders" are responsible for taking control or possession of the goods and products being shipped.

"Import-Export Broker": These are the coordinators and arrangers of importing and exporting. They work closely with the U.S. Customs offices, government regulatory offices, global carriers, and various other organizations and businesses that are involved in intercontinental freight transport.

"Agricultural Truck Broker": "Agricultural truck brokers" are typically a small company that operates exclusively in one geographic location in the country. If they are unregulated agricultural truck brokers, then they are responsible for arranging carrier services for agricultural products exempt from typical restrictions. They include things like raising livestock, forestry, cultivation of land, raising and harvesting any type of crops or aquatic resources, and more. You can read more about the Requirements for Exemption of Agricultural Industries here: https://www.irs.gov/charities-non-profits/other-non-profits/requirements-for-exemption-agricultural-horticultural-organization

"Shipper's Associations": The "shipper's associations" are exempt organizations, and typically operate as nonprofit. It allows them to combine their shipments with other shippers and that also cuts down on the number of trucks on the road. These associations function quite similarly to the "freight forwarders" with the exception of access. Only members of the association can access the shipper association's freight services.

ADVICE FOR BEGINNERS

If we lived in an ideal world, then each of these key influencers in the freight and transportation industry would fulfill only their specified roles and obligations. Unfortunately, the transportation industry is an ever-evolving beast and often the lines become blurred.

If you are successful, as I hope for you to be, then you may even grow large enough to expand your business with divisions or subsidiary companies. These subsidiaries may offer additional freight services in any of these traditional roles.

As you are starting out, my advice to you is to use as many of these organizations as possible in order to have a business that can meet a wider range of demands. These people will become your network of independent contractors that will represent you in their area of expertise.

This gives you, the broker, a presence in local communities that you might not otherwise have access to, and in turn, supplies the contractors with your freight brokerage service for their customers. It's a win/win.

As the brokerage firm, you are responsible for maintaining the surety bond and paying carriers and suppliers under this type of relationship with outside contractors in other areas of freight and transportation.

Education, Experience, and Training for Your New Journey

While this book is designed to give you as much information as possible in an easy to understand format, it is just the first start to learning how to begin your new home-based freight brokerage firm. It is not the entire education, experience, or training you will need to run and grow your business successfully. It is merely the start.

Education, experience, and training are what indicates success or failure as an entrepreneur. You need to understand not only the industry you want to start a business in, but what entrepreneurship is, and what it takes to become an entrepreneur. You can manage your 9-5 and work on your dreams at the same time.

The freight broker industry is much too competitive for you to rely on your own training or previous experience simply.

THE BEST ADVICE

When I started out my journey, I spoke to several successful brokers who were already moving tons of freight using a home-based business model.

The one thing they consistently mentioned was for me actually to work in the field before starting my own business. They suggested either working for a shipping company or a carrier or if there was a company that specialized in both that would be an ideal experience.

Don't spend hundreds or even thousands on a full-fledged training program. Go work for a company that offers its agents training for free, and use that knowledge and hands-on experience to start your own business. That was the advice given to me.

And I did just that.

I went to work for a local shipper/carrier, and I not only gained some valuable technical competence needed for this industry, but I also made contacts that helped me to jump-start my business when I was ready.

Several freight brokers in the industry choose to use independent agents or contractors, as I mentioned above in the shipper's association key player description. The agents represent the freight broker in a specific area of the country. This enables you to operate in an area where you would not have a justification for opening a new location or office.

One of the companies that I considered working with had agents in Florida, Georgia, Ohio, West Virginia, and Texas. They all worked from home, with no start-up costs, and a computer, telephone and fax machine. They were not freight brokers themselves, but merely an extension of the freight broker who held the bond.

WHAT I LEARNED

Some of the things I did as a freight agent include:

- Arranging the transportation and tracking of loads hauled by a particular freight company or carrier.

- Administrative support

- Matching carriers with customers' needs

- Sourcing carriers

- Dispatching trucks

- Scheduling deliveries and pick-ups

- Solving problems that could delay or damage a shipment.

This list just names a few of my responsibilities. While none of these tasks require a fancy college degree or an amazing amount of intellect, they do require you have a strong desire to follow through and keep diligent. These are important qualities to have in order to survive in this business.

CLASSES TO TAKE

In terms of general skills you need to have to run your own freight brokerage firm, I highly recommend you brush up on your math proficiency. You will be required to use this on a daily basis to negotiate rates, fees, and commissions.

Take some business courses on critical analysis and thinking. Learn to play chess if you don't already know how. You want to be able to see existing opportunities as they present themselves without having to reinvent the wheel to get anything done.

You will also need to take some communication courses and be comfortable interacting with people from all walks of life. 99% of your work will be done via remote communication like email and phone.

It's important to learn how to communicate effectively in both ways if you don't have much experience with negotiating or closing deals that way.

In addition to general business knowledge, you are also going to need to maintain current knowledge of the field. Make sure you read the top literature from experts in the industry.

Read as you are working in the industry so you can learn to apply your knowledge in real-world situations as you go along. That way, you have a better chance of not only honing in on that skill and perfecting it, but possibly coming up with ways to make it more succinct and effective for your own business.

PUBLICATIONS TO READ

I've done extensive research, reading thousands of white papers, eBooks, and hard copy books to get this education. I'm going to share the top 3 publications with you here, based on credibility and authority in the industry.

While these books are not free, I recommend you check them out as you can afford it and focus on one at a time. I'm going to list them in the order in which I read them myself, but by all means, read them in the order that makes sense for you and your goals.

There are tons of free resources on the web, which offer a great training element to them. I scoured just about all of them, trust me. I'll share the top 3 websites that I still refer to from time to time even after years of being in this industry.

1. LoadTraining - Free Books and Free Training – (https://loadtraining.com/freight-broker-training-kit/) LoadTraining prides itself on being the number one online freight broker training school. They offer one free video lesson and six complimentary books that guide you in your new freight brokerage journey. You can even learn how to make more money in the industry by analyzing market trends. You can also receive a guide on how to be a great freight broker.

2. I purchased the "Freight Broker Training Manual" (https://www.taltoa.com/) shortly after I completed reading the free guides from LoadTraining. You can purchase the digital copy for $49.95 or a hard copy for $69.95. Published by TALTOA Freight Broker Training and Consulting School. It is designed to go hand in hand with their live training. I opted to go for hands-on experience more than training, so I did not choose this option, but I still found the guide very useful for a start-up business, simply on its own merit.

3. Start Your Own Freight Brokerage Business, 5th Edition is where you can get all of your worksheets, templates, receipts, and agreements, as well as how to set your commission rates and find and hire employees for your home based business.

In order to become successful as a freight broker, you will need to possess a varying degree of skill sets. Some that take time to develop, others that you already have.

QUALITIES OF A GOOD TRAINING CURRICULUM

Taking freight broker classes is not a legal requirement to start your home-based business. They can be the initial foundation for your new career, should that be the best option for you. Everyone has different needs, learns differently, and experiences things in a different way, so I am not discouraging you from taking classes. I have found that I have been just as successful with the self-training and hands-on experience.

If you do choose to find your own school instead of using the one offered by the company you become an agent for, my recommendation is that you make sure they cover the following:

1. The basics of the industry and moving your first load

2. How to complete your applications and licensing requirements

3. Sponsor your BMC-84 broker bond (a prerequisite for your licensure)

4. How to use the freight broker software to automate processes like billing and orders

5. Cloned or original website assistance & set-up

The bottom line is that freight broker classes are designed to help some more than others. If you have a strong idea of where you need to improve, contact some of the local or online accredited and nationally recognized schools you prefer. Ask them if they offer personalized training and services that you specifically need. Sometimes they are willing to do that if you are willing to pay.

Much of the training classes will contain information you don't need to operate a home-based freight brokerage firm, so your diligence and research before spending money are well worth it.

SUGGESTED TRAINING CLASSES

- *Introduction to Transportation Systems*, a free course at MIT
- *Logistics Systems* also a free course at MIT

- Import and export training videos by the U.S. Census Bureau
- Export tutorials (globalEDGE) by Michigan State University

If you are interested in paying for more advanced training, review this list of the Top 5 Freight Broker Training Programs in the Country. (https://tinyurl.com/top5FBTraining)

As we have discussed, formal training is not necessary in order to open your freight broker business. Nothing beats hands-on training, but hands-on training or formal training is not for everyone, and that is totally ok.

Keeping up to date with the training and the educational aspect of the market is key once you have established yourself or how to get started on the right path as a new start-up. I've gathered the top resources for online training schools for freight brokers. Feel free to review each one, and find more on your own.

Brooke Transportation Training Solutions "One of the leading freight brokerage training schools online is offered through Brooke Transportation Training Solutions. The organization offers in-person classes in Texas, California, Florida, and North Carolina, but it also provides a comprehensive online training and career center. The courses give freight brokers a foundational education in operating a sound business, skills necessary for the job including communication and sales, as well as marketing guidance. Courses range in cost depending on the location and the reach of the training."

Transport Training International "Transport Training International offers a variety of freight broker training classes both online and in-classroom, with downloadable materials and interactive training modules. The company stands out as an online resource for several reasons, including the fact that thousands of brokers have completed its training and the company provides ongoing support post-graduation. Transport Training International also offers guaranteed freight broker placement for those who want to work as an independent broker after completing the training."

American Broker Academy "The Seattle, Washington-based American Broker Academy is a well-known training resource for new and established freight brokers. It offers a variety of courses aimed at helping freight brokers stay compliant with regulation changes, understanding how to operate a business, negotiating rates, and communicating with customers. There are classes available at the Seattle location, but also several online courses and articles for those who prefer to learn remotely."

JPL Enterprises "Based in Florida, JPL Enterprises International operates a transportation management consulting firm that provides strategic training to freight brokers. Through educational DVDs, live in-person classes, and training-on-demand services, JPL is one of the most comprehensive freight broker training resources available online. The company also provides many articles relevant to the freight brokerage business that allows for individual education at one's own pace."

JW Bond Consultants "JW Surety Bonds also offers resources for freight brokers online, including an all-encompassing e-book on establishing a freight brokerage business as well as an up-to-date list of the top 12 freight broker training programs. The surety bond agency also provides several online resources to freight brokers above and beyond educational requirements, including bond pricing information, how to assess training programs, and how to operate a successful freight broker business."

Study.com "While Study.com is not specifically geared toward freight brokers like some of the other online resources listed here, the website has several training programs available for free that are relevant to brokers in the business. The education institution offering the class organizes the majority of the courses listed on the site, and nearly all are available at no cost."

Regulatory Resources ""In addition to formal freight broker schools and training programs, it is necessary for brokers to keep up to date with regulatory changes and trends in the industry. The Department of Transportation offers some resources online, as does the Federal Motor Carrier Safety Administration. Some leading industry blogs also provide information and insight into upcoming changes to regulations relevant to freight brokers."

Online Articles and Forums "Blogs and freight broker forums can be invaluable online tools for new and established freight brokers. Some articles available online offer industry insights along with best practices in the ever-changing landscape of the business, while online forums allow for the easy connection with industry professionals. Checking in with these resources regularly helps freight brokers stay abreast of important information in the business."

Online training programs and resources can make all the difference in creating and sustaining a successful freight broker business.

Next, let's talk about what a typical day in the life of a freight broker looks like.

Freight Brokerage Daily Operations

As a home-based freight broker, from the moment your eyes open and your feet touch the floor, you are going to have fast-paced days full of adrenaline and high pressure.

It's extremely exciting and lucrative, to say the least. There are days where you won't be thanked, and you will feel a little stressed, but that's normal. It's totally ok, as long as you know how to channel that energy.

HYPOTHETICAL SCENARIO: A TYPICAL WORK DAY

So, here is what a typical workday might be like.

Your day begins as the alarm goes off at 6:00 am. You're brushing your teeth, making coffee or tea, and it's go-time!

You step into your office, turn on the light, your computers, your printer, and your fax machine. Open the blinds, so when the sun comes out it automatically shines in the office.

You can then turn off the overhead light and work by sunlight. Especially if you get good lighting in your home office.

Settle in your chair, sip your hot coffee, sit back and open up your voicemail. Check all your voicemails from the previous day and write down those you need to call back, take action on, email, or follow up with at a later time.

The voicemails you will have are mostly going to be from your carriers letting you know the status of their loads, any delays or accidents, anything else that you need to know as you start your day. It's wise to prioritize those things first.

Organize the information in a way that will help you tackle it in order of urgency and preference. Set up any reminders you need for yourself as you go along. Google calendar is a simple way to get reminders 30 minutes before an event via email and desktop notification.

Next, clear off your new faxes on the fax machine, or if you use an online fax service, check your email, which is where they will typically be.

What you will get via fax are confirmations for your loads, BOLs (Bill of Ladings), and tons of other information that you are going to find invaluable as you go about your day.

You will occasionally get some junk so simply recycle it and keep what you need. Get folders and a filing cabinet to easily organize and keep your faxes. We will talk more about that in further detail when we talk about your home office set-up.

The next thing you will want to do is call any of your carriers that are still on the road and delivering shipments. Since this industry operates on just about a 24 hour day 7 days a week, you won't have any problems reaching drivers that early in the morning. In fact, they prefer the contact at the start of their day, instead of in the middle of the afternoon when trying to get a load dropped off.

Get all the information you need from each driver on the road in one phone call. If your shipper or the person receiving the order happens to call during the day to check on the status of delivery, you have answers for them.

The most important thing you want to ask each carrier is their ETA for each load, and information about the cargo itself.

When you go to check your emails, you have all the information you need to respond to them quickly and easily without a ton of research, waiting, or lag time.

Your morning will be reserved to work through all of your appointments, have a status on all schedules for your carriers, and confirm that all shipments from the day before have been delivered satisfactorily with no damages or missing items.

By mid-morning you should be famished! Whew! That was a lot of work, right? Take some time to have breakfast to feed your brain.

When you come back, get ready to check your boards for what is coming up for delivery that day, and find out what equipment and trucks are available to get things moving.

As your day goes on, you will start to get incoming calls from your carriers.

CASE EXAMPLE: BROKERING A SHIPMENT

Mark, a new driver of yours in Florida, who operates as an Independent Contractor/owner-operator of "Mark's Transportation Company, LLC," calls you in hopes that you have some extra freight he can backhaul. Mark wants to make up for one of his other loads canceling on him. It happens.

As you check your orders, you discover that you just read an email from one of your shippers asking for a last minute haul. So you ask Mark what he needs to make at a minimum on the load. You tell him to give you 10 minutes to make some calls.

You call the shipper, confirming a rate for the shipment that allows you to pay Mark his rate, while making a profit yourself, of course.

You confirm all the details with both parties and begin the necessary documentation to start the load life.

Because Mark is already an agent of yours, you have a standing agreement in place, as you do with all of your carriers and shippers.

The first thing you want to do is confirm the rate agreed upon with the shipper and send them a shipper rate confirmation that requires their signature and return.

You can get this free rate confirmation form here: Rate Confirmation Sheet https://www.sampletemplates.com/business-templates/sheet/rate-sheet-templates.html

Shipper		Consignee	
Name:	_____	Name:	_____
Address:	_____	Address:	_____
City/State/Zip:	_____	City/State/Zip:	_____
Pickup # / Misc:	_____		
Pickup Date/Time:	_____	Delivery Appointment:	_____

If you are interested in our "Quick Pay" program please call 412.788.8878 Option 1 for more information or check a box and sign below:	Stop/Pickup City/ State
4% Same Day ☐	_____
3% Next Day ☐	_____
Signature: _____	_____

Additional Information:
_____
_____
_____
_____
_____

Commodity: _____		TARP REQUIRED ☐ YES ☐ NO	
Approx. Weight: _____		EQUIPMENT _____	
Rate To Carrier: _____		Driver : _____	
Accessorials:		Carrier: _____	
Description	*Carrier Pay*	Carrier Phone: _____	
_____	_____	Carrier Fax: _____	
_____	_____	Carrier/Clearance # _____	
_____	_____	or MC # _____	

American Transport Dispatching Terminal Information:

Charges may be assessed to carrier for late pickup or delivery! Carrier must still adhere to all Hours of Service regulations.

Terminal Phone = _____
Terminal Fax = _____
Terminal Contact _____

Carrier send invoice to: American Transport, Inc.
100 Industry Drive
Pittsburgh, PA 15275

ORIGINAL PAPERWORK MUST
ACCOMPANY INVOICE!

ABSOLUTELY NO DOUBLE-BROKERING
It is agreed that any re-brokering of this load will result in non-payment to carrier, in addition to any other penalties applicable by contract or by law.

CARRIER SIGN AND RETURN TO ABOVE FAX NUMBER

Authorized Carrier Signature : _____

Image Provided by SampleTemplates.com

To schedule the shipment, you must collect the following information on every shipment. This is standard operating procedure for freight brokers.

- Names and addresses of the consignor and consignee

- Pick-up and delivery address

- Commodity

- Dispatch Telephone Number

- Delivery Time

- Total Miles

You are going to have to provide all of these details to Mark, your carrier, so he can accurately provide a quote and accept the load.

Mark's Transportation Company, LLC has agreed to transport the freight to Kissimmee, Florida, 600 miles away, for a flat fee of $1300 for delivery.

They are charging you about $2.10 a mile, which is not bad considering all of the circumstances surrounding this particular load. It might otherwise have cost close to $3.50 per mile with another carrier.

We caught Mark in a bind, so he's willing to lower his rate to go home. Why would Mark do this? So he isn't leaving empty handed!

You have communicated with your shipper, who has confirmed the availability of the cargo. You have also confirmed with Mark, Your carrier, that he is ready to accept the load and can get it all the way to its destination.

You are going to owe Mark $1300 for his delivery fee, and your cut is going to vary based on what you have already worked out with that particular shipping company. A typical broker will earn anywhere from 15-20% in commission according to state and industry regulations and laws.

During each transport, you make sure everything is going smoothly by often communicating with your carriers and your recipients.

WHAT ELSE HAPPENS IN A TYPICAL DAY?

Check your email and the board throughout the day. Be sure to answer any calls during your business hours so you can stay on top of your customer's shipments and loads.

Check the fax machine.

At the end of your day, whatever time you have set your office hours, enjoy time off because you will rinse and repeat the next business day.

Next time, Mark might be Stacey, and there might be another more pressing concern than just picking up a backhaul.

Each day will bring new adventures, so if you love variety, this is definitely the career choice for you.

I've made your day seem extremely simple, which it typically is as a home-based business model.

Software Needed to Run Your Business

There is a variety of specific software that you will need in order to get things done properly and according to industry regulations and standards.

The freight brokers that I know have learned to master the art of multi-tasking and juggling many things at one time.

From dispatching your freight, finding carriers, tracking client shipments, processing contractor and agent payroll, following up with invoices, there's a lot to juggle in a typical day.

So how do you keep it all in the air? Software.

As mentioned before, the freight broker business is fast-paced. You will need to invest in freight management software in order to let it do all of the juggling.

How do you decide which one is best? That all depends on what your business goals, individual goals, and needs are, as well as your budget.

The main software that you need is officially called "TMS, Transportation Management Software." It will help you streamline your entire load process from start to finish, which allows you to scale and grow.

I've compiled a list of the most trusted software in the business so that you can run your freight brokerage firm from any location on any device without lengthy contracts.

TMS SOFTWARE OPTIONS

Load Pilot: www.loadpilot.com

Load Pilot software allows you to quote, book, organize, manage your freight loads. It has an easy to use interface that lets you integrate faxing or email services for quicker invoicing. You can get an at-a-glance overview of daily and weekly load activities. It even comes with access to their master database of over 160 thousand carriers all over the U.S. It includes a personal accounting ledger, calendar, and much more.

Strategy Systems: www.strategysystems.com

With easy integration with QuickBooks, Strategy Systems software allows you to dispatch freight, incorporate fuel tax for your carriers, complete billing and payroll, get driver and dispatch records, track shipments, and monitor maintenance on your equipment and trucks.

Aljex & Descartes: https://www.aljex.com

This flexible software is perfect for you, just starting out as a home-based business. It is flexible enough to grow with you. You can automate a ton of your daily routine tasks with this software, allowing you to simplify your accounting activities. You can view all of your shipments in one easy to navigate platform, and manage commonly used documents and templates.

3PL Systems: http://3plsystems.com/

This is a typical software with all the normal tools that TMS software has to help you run your business more efficiently. There's also a nifty customer dashboard that allows your clients to track their own shipments. This way, you can avoid those daily interruptions and phone calls, putting the power in your customer's hands. This feature can be a great added benefit to doing business with you. There's also a sales dashboard that you can use for your in-house sales team to help them automate quotes, dispatch freight loads, and track your freight shipments.

Rose Rocket: https://www.roserocket.com/

If real-time data and transparency across your organization is your number one priority, then Rose Rocket is the software for you. You can see your shipment details as they happen, watch invoices be paid in real time, and chat with your drivers via a live chat feature. It includes a mobile app which is available for download. The interface is quite modern and simplistic. This software works for any size freight brokerage firm.

Ascend TMS: https://ascendtms.com/signup

Unlike the rest of the TMS Software above, Ascend is also an SCM (supply chain management) software. It is ideal whether you are a startup or have 1000's of agents across the country. The GPS feature allows you to track your shipments in real time on an interactive map. There is also a driver payroll dashboard that gives you flexibility when paying drivers based on their preference - paid per mile, per hour, per pallet, or even per ton.

SOFTWARE SELECTION ADVICE

Take time to connect with the live chat reps on these and other sites that you have researched. Ask for a demo before you make any purchase. Most of the time, you can see a demo right on the company website.

Look for ones that offer a free trial so you have time to try it out before you buy it to make sure it's going to be what you need and what you can grow into.

Look for a software program that will simplify your life and is easy to use. It should automate many of the processes you would have to do manually as a solo practice from home.

It is imperative that you do your research examine all the available options, not just the ones listed here. Many of the TSM software options do not include a load board, so you will need to find software that integrates with your load board software.

Let's examine the life of a load so you understand what is involved from start to finish. You can begin to make a note of the bare minimum functions you would like your software to have.

The Life of a Freight Load and Your Role

STEP 1: THE ORDER

A shipping company will email or call the freight broker, you, to pick up a load of cargo in a specific location. As the freight broker, you must gather all of the necessary information. Here is what you need to gather.

Customer Information

Company Name

Point of Contact

Email

Phone

Shipper Information

Name

Address

Point of Contact

Email

Phone

Hours, including shift change

| How to Schedule Pick-up | Phone/email/online portal |

Customer Information

Name

Address

Point of Contact

Email

Phone

Hours, including shift
change

How to Schedule Delivery	Phone/email/online portal

Order Information

Reference
Numbers for
Shipper

There could be multiple reference numbers - Purchase Order (PO), Pick Up (PU), Invoice, or Confirmation numbers.

Reference
Numbers for
Consignee

There could be multiple numbers here, too - Purchase Order (PO), Delivery, Invoice, or Confirmation numbers.

Ready Date

Must Arrive
by Date
(MABD)

Acceptable
Range for
Pick-Up Date

Acceptable
Range for
Delivery
Date

Product
Commodity

Equipment
Type

Freight Class   *Only required for LTL shipments*

Net Weight

Gross Weight

Number
Cases or
Pieces

Pallet
Dimensions

Whether
Pallets are
Stackable

Hazardous
Code

Special
Require-
ments

Temperature
Range

If you are using software that allows your shippers to access the portal directly, then there is no need for them to email you or call you. The shipper simply enters their shipping information into the software to be processed and transmitted to the carrier automatically.

STEP 2: SCHEDULING THE FREIGHT OR CARGO

Once you have received the details above from the shipper, either in the software automatically or via email/phone, it is your role to schedule the pickup. Confirm the details of the order and coordinate the drop-off and pick up time.

As a freight broker, your services provide extreme value to the freight industry. Your job is securing quality transportation for cargo through negotiation and booking loads that a carrier can then transport.

It is crucial that you take time to build your network of vetted carriers that you can rely upon. Utilize a truck broker to help you find the right carriers, as they have access to thousands of contacts at a time.

Before actually scheduling a load, you must verify that the carrier or trucking company has the following important features, at a minimum:

- A truck that is neat and tidy and up to code

- A valid driver's license

- The required amount of liability insurance coverage

- Flexibility to handle special requirements

- A trailer free of contaminated or hazardous materials

- Availability during the transport times that you need them.

STEP 3: DISPATCHING THE ORDER

Here is where the fun begins! You will get a chance to try out your fancy new TMS software. When you get an order via email, phone, fax, or automatically through your software, you will then need to reach out to your list of drivers quickly.

Double check their information like the company name, the type of trailer or truck they have, the trailer number of your shipment, the truck number, the cell phone and direct office line of the driver, and the driver's current location.

You will then communicate all of the specific requirements of the shipment, which will also be given to the driver when he picks up the order/load.

STEP 4: THE LOADING

You will need to stay in constant contact with the driver/carrier during the entire process and even more so during the loading.

Your shipment is not considered to be complete until all of the cargo has been loaded into the truck/trailer and the trailer has been sealed. The shipper is then given a BOL (Bill of Lading) to sign where they accept responsibility for the load at that point.

Whenever you speak to your carrier or driver, you will need to verify all of the order inventory and the destination of the load that appears on the BOL. Make sure the correct cargo will arrive at your client.

You do not want to have to try and go back and figure out what happened to a wrong load, as that would cost a lot of time and money.

STEP 5: TRANSPORTING THE LOAD

As a freight broker, you will want to look at tracking software. On example would be "Macro Point" https://www.macropoint.com/ which enables your drivers with GPS. This allows you to track each shipment down to the minute.

Regularly checking in with your drivers also ensures that the shipment is on track to be delivered on time and to the right location.

You will want to consider providing your drivers with directions, helping them to navigate traffic and weather problems that might cause a delay in the shipment.

STEP 6: DELIVERING THE LOAD AND UNLOADING IT

Once the cargo/freight has reached the intended location, the shipper is required to write down what time they arrived.

This is just in case there is ever an issue with detainment. If the driver waits too long, they could be charged a detention fee.

When the driver has unloaded the entire shipment, the receiver will then sign the BOL. They will denote anything wrong with the shipment, finalize the acceptance of the load, and document the time they received it.

You will then need to wait on the driver/carrier to return with the paperwork. Once you have the paperwork, you can then invoice the shipper, and in turn, can pay your driver.

STEP 7: BILLING THE LOAD

To bill the client, you will need to receive the paperwork from your driver. This includes the invoice along with all of the other paperwork he/she has in their possession, such as the BOL and Proof of delivery.

Once you have all of this documentation, then the shipper is ready to be billed officially, and an invoice can be sent to them for payment.

As the freight broker, you are an indispensable part of the trucking industry. Your job helps take many tasks off the plate of shippers and carriers.

Developing your expertise and staying in constant communication with your network is the foundation and keys to your success.

So now that you understand what a freight broker does and what is involved in the day to day operations, let's dive into the legalities of starting your freight brokerage firm from home.

Chapter II: Federal Requirements for Freight Brokerage Firms

Federal Motor Carrier Safety Administration

Courtesy of truckinginfo.com

All freight brokers, regardless of whether operating from home or out of a brick and mortar building, need to stay on top of all the new rules and regulations of the industry.

Keeping up with regulations and renewing your bond during the correct renewal period is critical. Maintaining these standards saves you valuable time and money.

Below is a list of the main basic compliance requirements you are going to need to obtain and maintain in order to operate your freight broker business.

I've provided resources where appropriate to cut down on your research time. Let's start with the basic Federal requirements for freight brokers.

Federal Compliance Requirements for Freight Brokers

The "Code of Federal Regulations (CFR), Part - 371 - Brokers of Property" is the set of laws that regulates the freight industry. There are several requirements that freight brokers need to adhere to, as well as a set of special rules and regulations for those who ship household goods and products.

As the freight broker industry grows and steadily increases, so do the number of licensed freight brokers in the United States. At the start of 2015, there were over 15 thousand licensed freight brokers in the industry. Later in the same year, there were more than 16 thousand.

By January of 2017, there were a record number of licensed brokers in the US at 17 thousand. That means the outlook for this industry is steadily increasing, and you are choosing to enter it at a time of amazing growth and profitability.

STEP 1: REGISTER WITH THE STATE AND IRS

The process for you to become licensed starts with registering your business in the state where you are going to operate. Since this is a home based business model, you will want to register in the state in which you reside.

Each state has its own set of procedures for registering your business. Make sure you check your Secretary of State website for the specific rules and filing fees. Here is a compiled list of Secretary of State website information https://www.thebalancesmb.com/secretary-of-state-websites-1201005

Once you have filed your business registration with the state, you will want to get an EIN (Employer

Identification Number from the IRS), so you can have a proper business tax registration.

If you also plan on providing the carrier service, as some freight brokers do, then you will also need to visit your local transportation agency.

Part of registering your business will involve determining the type of structure your business will have.

Corporation, Partnership, Sole Proprietorship, and LLC (Limited Liability Company) are your business structure options. There is no right or wrong decision when it comes to the set-up of your business. Check out this article on Entrepreneur.com that breaks down each type of business structure.

Several factors determine which type of business structure to use Consider whether or not you are starting the business alone or with partners, and if you want your personal assets kept separate from business liability.

Always reach out to your local Small Business Administration to help you decide what option is best for you.

STEP 2: REGISTER YOUR FREIGHT BROKER LICENSE WITH URS (UNIFIED REGISTRATION SYSTEM)

Prior to December 12, 2015, new freight brokers were required to also register with the FMCSA, the Federal Motor Carrier Safety Administration.

While the new process was designed to streamline the application while putting all the required forms in one portal, it can still be tough figuring out a new system.

The FMCSA offers free training to help you step by step through the application process for FREE. Free training offered by the FMCSA (https://portal.fmcsa.dot.gov/urstraining/index.html)

STEP 3: COMPLETE THE OPERATING AUTHORITY APPLICATION

One of the very first things you will need to do when applying for your license is to also apply for an operating authority (https://www.fmcsa.dot.gov/registration/get-mc-number-authority-operate). This is also known as the MC number.

This number and your "operating authority" are just what they sound like. This is your authority to operate this freight brokerage firm from home.

You can choose from 2 different types of operating authorities as a freight broker. Which type you choose is going to be dependent upon the types of cargo that you will be transporting and arranging.

You do not have to choose one over the other. If you choose to operate as both authorities, you allow yourself room for more income.

Each application will need to have the fee paid and will be discussed in Chapter III.

The two types of operating authority are:

1. Property Freight Brokers

2. Household Good Freight Brokers

If you also want to offer carrier services in your freight brokerage firm, you will need to visit the United States Department of Transportation and obtain a USDOT number (https://www.fmcsa.dot.gov/registration/do-i-need-usdot-number) as well.

You do not have to decide to become both authorities at once. Take your time and do what's best for you and what you can manage on your own.

STEP 4: GET YOUR MC/FF NUMBER AND GRANT AWARD

After you have submitted your application, you will get an MC/FF number. FF numbers are assigned to freight broker designations, and the MC number is for all other carriers and brokers. The type of authority you have applied for will determine if you get just one or both of these numbers.

This is one of the most vital pieces of information about your business. You will want to keep this number safe, secure, and easily accessible at all times.

I memorized mine. Why? Because this is the number that is used by the insurers who are filing paperwork on behalf of your business with the FMCSA.

Keep in mind, this number is not your operating authority, and your application is not considered complete until you have received your official grant award by certified mail.

This award is the certification/documentation of your MC/FF number and proof that you are now in possession of it, officially. While the grant letter is being sent to you, your operating authority application is going to be published in the FMCSA Register.

This publication starts a 10-day countdown period where you have to wait for your application for operating authority to be challenged. This challenge can be by any person or company who thinks that you should not be given this authority and want to stop it.

If you have never been in this industry and don't owe people money from a previous business, then you should be just fine.

STEP 5: GETTING YOUR FREIGHT BROKER SURETY BOND/TRUST AGREEMENT

While you are waiting for your 10-day protest period to count down, you do not have to sit on your hands. I highly recommend that you start doing research on finding the bond company that will issue you your surety bond.

The BMC-84 bond is the bond required to start a freight brokerage firm. It offers the financial protection for you and the clients that you serve. It basically is a guarantee that if you do not follow all laws and regulations, or if you cause any damage or loss to a company, that they have a legal right to file a claim against your bond to recover their losses.

The BMC-84 Bond is $75,000 in value, which is now a minimum requirement as of October 1, 2013. The bond must be obtained from a licensed and reputable surety bond agency. These are the agencies that will work on your behalf with the bond issuers and backers.

The amount with which you can obtain your bond is going to be dependent upon your credit score, your finances, and other financial factors.

You will receive a quote based on those factors. For those with good credit, hat quote typically ranges anywhere from 1-5% of the total bond amount

Please, don't panic! My credit was not that great either when I applied to become a freight broker. I worked with companies that specialize in getting freight brokers bonded and insured under unusual circumstances.

Lance Surety is one of these companies. They do not require any collateral down payments to get started. You have 90 days total to get your bond when your application has officially been published with the FMCSA register. Do not let that time get away from you.

Once you have found a company to issue you a bond, as required by law, they will automatically file all necessary documents with the FMCSA on your behalf. You will get copies of the filing for your records.

In regards to selecting a bond company, do your research. This research should be based on your credit score and how much of a bond you need or can afford to purchase to start your business.

Keep in mind other expenses like your software, purchasing freight broker insurance, and if you plan on getting your carrier or forward authority as well.

Here are three of the top surety bond companies based on credibility and price.

1. JW Bond Consultants Inc. (888) 592-6631- http://www.jwsuretybonds.com

2. Bryant Surety Bonds, Inc. (866) 450-3412 - http://www.bryantsuretybonds.com

3. Pacific Financial Inc. (800) 595-2615 -
http://www.pac-fin.com

STEP 6: OBTAINING FREIGHT BROKER INSURANCE

It is a federal law that all freight brokers hold freight broker insurance if they plan on operating as a freight carrier and forwarder as well. If you are only operating as the broker, you do not have to obtain insurance.

You will want to get cargo insurance as a broker. This way, if there is damage to a shipment, it's not taken out of your bond. It is also recommended you get general liability and property insurance coverage as well.

If you are going to hire employees in your business and pay taxes on them, you will need to obtain workers compensation insurance for each employee. You will need to be verified with your State.

Your carriers are going to need to have workers' compensation insurance themselves, even if you do, too. If they happen to be exempt, they can provide you with a written statement for your records, so you are covered.

FMCSA Regulation 49 CFR Part 366 is the law that requires all freight brokers to list each process agent that they are going to use in each state that they have an office in or plan to write contracts and do business in.

You can be your own agent for the state where you live and operate your home based freight brokerage firm.

Once the 10-day protest period has ended and there have been no objections to your application, the FMCSA will officially issue your freight broker license. This is also your operating authority.

Congratulations! You are now a licensed freight brokerage firm! But before you pull out the cigars, let's keep going with your requirements so you can KEEP your authority.

Record Keeping and Accurate Accounting Requirements

The FMCSA and the Department of Transportation are the regulatory bodies that oversee this industry. They require that each freight broker keep accurate records of each and every single transaction, which is each shipment/load, for a period of up to three years.

Each record must contain the name, address, and phone number of the sellers, shippers, and carriers. You will also need to keep each BOL (Bill of Lading), as well as how much you were paid for your services for each load.

The records will need to be kept in a place where each party of the transaction can access them at any given time. Look for software that offers document storage as a feature. This will help you keep everything in one place.

Misrepresenting Yourself as a Carrier

The CFR (Code of Federal Regulations), § 371.7 Section on Misrepresentation, states:

" **(a)** A broker shall not perform or offer to perform any brokerage service (including advertising), in any name other than that in which its registration is issued.

(b) A broker shall not, directly or indirectly, represent its operations to be that of a carrier. Any advertising shall show the broker status of the operation.

[45 FR 68942, Oct. 17, 1980. Redesignated at 61 FR 54707, Oct. 21, 1996, as amended at 62 FR 15421, Apr. 1, 1997]"

This means that you cannot let anyone believe that you are functioning as a broker and carrier if you do not have the carrier authority assigned to you.

Any advertisement that you create, any marketing that you do, must make it clear that you are performing brokerage services only and not carrier services unless you actually are and licensed to do so.

You are only permitted to use the business name that you have registered with the authority and the state and are not permitted to use DBAs to offer different freight broker services.

You can learn more at the FMCSA website on misrepresentation (https://www.fmcsa.dot.gov/).

Charging Carriers for Services

Now, I'm not here to burst your bubble, but it's important to tell you about how NOT to charge your services in order to avoid complications and potential legal situations.

One of the major things that is a huge "no-no" in this industry is shipping your own goods/cargo then charging a carrier for performing the brokerage services that are associated with the delivery or transportation of the load.

You also are not permitted to give your carriers anything of value. You may give them free or relatively cheap marketing materials that you have purchased on their behalf, but that is about it. Buying gifts for carriers is construed as buying influence.

Rules for Different Goods Shipped

For shipment of household goods, the CFR includes an entirely separate section of rules for these types of cargo. The rules relating to household goods can be quite cumbersome.

It is highly advised that freight brokers interested in getting started with this type of authority read the entire Subchapter B, Part 371 of the CFR to become familiar with all the requirements and regulations.

Food Safety Regulations and Laws

In 2016, the Food and Drug Administration issued a rule regarding the transportation of human and animal food. This rule came into effect in April 2017.

This rule only applies to shippers and brokerage firms who have more than 500 employees and are shipping more than $27 million dollars in loads per year.

Brokers must still comply with this rule to ensure that all of their network and employees are in compliance. They also must clearly define procedures and company policies about how they will manage the compliance of the laws regarding food safety.

The FDA has released a "Small Entity Compliance Guide" available on their website, for you to review and gain further insight for compliance of your new business (https://www.fda.gov/regulatory-information/search-fda-guidance-documents/small-entity-compliance-guide-sanitary-transportation-human-and-animal-food-what-you-need-know-about).

Bond Renewal Laws

In order to remain compliant and in business, you will need to mark your calendar with two extremely important renewal dates. These are your FMCSA information and your freight broker bond.

FMCSA Registration and Authority Renewal/Update

Whenever you have a change in any of the following, you must notify the FMCSA.

- Your business designation or registration
- The status of your operating authority, adding a new authority, or removing an authority
- Insurance policy limits and terms
- Equipment and location changes

If you are also operating as a carrier or shipper, you will need to update the USDOT records as well.

Aside from changes, you are required to keep in touch with the authoritative agencies every 2 years. Thirty days before you are due for an update, they will send out a friendly reminder via postal mail.

FREIGHT BROKER BOND RENEWAL

Freight broker bonds will need to be renewed each year on the anniversary of its effective date of surety.

If you do not renew your freight broker bond, you will be in violation of the laws and compliance regulations set forth by the FMCSA. That could result in your license being revoked or suspended.

It can also be revoked for repeat instances to renew and failure to maintain it consistently.

An important note is that you will want to renew your bond no longer than 30 days before the expiration date.

In order to remain compliant, you are going to need to be conscientious of the myriad of federal regulations that are for freight brokers in the industry.

You will hear about these in detail during your training, but I highly recommend that you review Subchapter B-Part 371, of Title 49, which describes the CFR (Code of Federal Regulations) regarding requirements.

THREE MAIN GENERAL REQUIREMENTS

If you keep in mind the three general requirements of every freight broker, then you are off to a healthy start with a solid foundation.

1. Keep accurate and easily accessible records
2. Do not misrepresent yourself
3. Keep proper accounting records in the operation of your business or hire a CPA

There are numerous consequences for non-compliance, none of which you want to find out about. The most significant consequence is a claim against your freight broker bond.

Do your research, stay compliant, stay in business, and you stay in the black.

Chapter III: The Cost of Doing Business and the Time Required to Run a Home-based Freight Brokerage Firm

Now that you know what is involved in the day to day operations, federal requirements, and how to manage your freight brokerage business, it's time to discuss the cost to even open your doors.

Start-Up Costs

How much is it going to cost you exactly?

There is no exact measure to determine that figure down to the dollar, but I will attempt to give you a ballpark figure.

There are several costs that you are going to incur at the start of your business. These costs include:

- Your business registration fees which can range from $150.00 to $300.00

- Your operating authority fees of $300 per authority

- One-time UCR registration fee of $76

- Freight broker bond fees, $900 to $3,000 annually

- Insurance policy fees of about $1,200 to $1,500 annually

- Worker's compensation, up to $3,000

- TMS software costs about $600 to $1,200 annually

- Miscellaneous business equipment costs

    - Phone line, $100 to $300

    - Office Supplies, up to $500

- Optional training fees, Free to $5,000

- Variable marketing and advertising costs

There is no one price that you can expect to pay for any of these services.

Fees vary by state for business registrations. Your credit score and your cargo will determine your insurance rates and bond fees, etc.

The cost of your bond is going to be on a case-by-case basis. As we discussed earlier, the bond cost is based on your credit score, your experience in the industry, and your financial trustworthiness.

The agency you choose to do business with will also play a factor in the cost. The price listed above is if you have nearly perfect credit.

The breakdown of the bond rate can be explained as follows:

Credit	Excellent	Good	Bad
Bond Rate	1.2-3%	3-5%	5-10%
Est. Cost	$900-2,250	$2,250-3,750	$3,750-7,500

The prices that bond companies charge are ever-changing phenomena in the industry. Prices change due to the market, competition, losses, and more.

The best way to ensure you get a lower rate is by working with a company that represents more than one surety bond company. This way, they can easily compare rates for you in-house.

COMMON START-UP ESSENTIALS

To find the cost of these start-up essentials, please visit some of the sites below. This is not an all-inclusive list, so please do your own research to make sure you have enough information to consider all of your options.

- Load board subscriptions
  - o Internet Truckstop
    http://www.truckstop.com
  - o TransCore 360 Express
    http://express.transcore.com
- Dispatch software
  - o ITS Dispatch http://www.itsdispatch.com
  - o Dr. Dispatch -
    http://www.drdispatch.com

ADDITIONAL OFFICE EXPENSE SUGGESTIONS

RingCentral: RingCentral offers small businesses the type of world-class business functionality that, until recently, was available only to large corporations (http://www.ringcentral.com).

Constant Contact: Email marketing is a very cost-effective method for a business to market its products or services to a broad audience. Often, you will already have your own email list you have compiled from your client base.

http://www.constantcontact.com

Expectations and Commitments

I would like to take this opportunity to be as transparent as possible about this next topic.

Understanding the expectations and commitments of the business is the most important quality to be able to maintain and grow the success you build.

Of course, my intention is not to discourage you in any way, after emboldening you in the first two chapters.

While this is an extremely lucrative business to run, it is more than just filling out applications and watching the fax machine for new orders. It must also be run properly by the rules and regulations surrounding the industry.

It's not even about buying a bunch of equipment just to be able to write it off on your taxes.

Before you even start your own firm, if you decide to go to work for an already established brokerage firm to obtain hands-on experience, then you are going to be able to build your book of business.

While you will get some business from the contacts you made while working for another firm, it's going to be very little.

The businesses you have established relationships with are going to do what any smart business owner would do. They are going to keep their relationships with their current carriers, brokers, shippers, and agents intact, while giving you a portion that none of them wanted, or will miss.

They do this just to see if you can handle it.

Can you blame them? You are leaving an established broker to start your own home based brokerage firm. They want to make sure you can handle what they are accustomed to getting in terms of service and deliverability.

Fair enough. Actions speak louder than words. You can show them better than you can tell them!

Let's say you opted to go with the free TMS software version until things start to ramp up.

What will you do if the client wants detailed reporting and integrations? How will you provide them with recent insurance information and carrier details that you have negotiated? What will you do if you have not set up the rate with the carriers yet and they want to know rates that you haven't obtained?

Unless you get up to speed, you are going to go out of business before you even start.

STAY ORGANIZED

How are you going to keep it together? Organization.

Choosing the wrong type of infrastructure can make or break your new home-based freight brokerage firm. I'm referring to specifically how you manage your documents, billing, and your account practices.

We've already discussed what TMS (Transportation Management Software) software is. It keeps you from dropping any balls during your daily juggling routine. The software is designed to centralize everything that goes on in your day-to-day operations.

Wasted time is one of the biggest reasons for failure in this industry. It's also why freight brokerage firms find themselves unable to grow past the start-up stage.

At some point, you are going to get things under control. Your business is going to grow steadily.

TIPS FOR MANAGING EMPLOYEES

It's at that point you will want to hire more people to help you. How are you going to manage them?

Even if you have prior management experience and consider yourself to be a stellar manager, it is not as easy as it looks. You must find and hire the right people for your freight brokerage firm, people who you can work well with and trust.

There is no class that you can take to make you a perfect manager. Learning how to be a good manager is no easy feat.

However, there are several things you can do to make managing your employees the optimal experience for you, for them, and your business.

Finding a TMS that allows you to segment and separate department logins and access is the start. Provide each of your employees with logins that limit their access to sensitive client information, or information about the business, that is not essential for their role.

For example, Jason in sales doesn't need access to your rate sheet. Likewise, Allison from accounting does not need to see the entire business plan, only the portions that are relevant to her and accounting.

It's no secret that sales teams are sharks in deep, infested waters, and you, my friend, are the dolphin.

Guarding your contacts and salespeople from each other will save you a lot of heartache in the long run. It also ensures that your sales agents cannot simply up and take off with your contacts, just as you did when you left the established brokerage firm.

Your TMS software will help you segregate your contacts and access to your contact list. You can ensure that each salesperson only has access to their own leads and contacts.

This ensures Jason can't go in and browse through Sally's contacts and start calling them when he as a not so profitable day with his own contacts.

SOME SOBERING ADVICE

If this were really super easy, as some might have you believe, then everyone would be operating a freight brokerage firm from home.

The reality is, this is not for everyone.

It takes a lot of time and commitment to manage all of the moving parts of this business. Your duties include keeping cargo on the road, trucks full of shipments, and maintaining your profit margin at a level that allows you to remain in business.

These roadblocks are just a few of the things you need to stay committed to and can potentially expect to happen in your business.

Technology changes daily, and it's up to us and our network to keep up with those changes while keeping our clients satisfied and coming back.

Focus on the technology that will help you stand out from your competition and set you up for long term success. That also includes keeping up with the relationships you foster and establish.

Financial Relationships That Matter

There are many relationships you need to establish in this business. There are two relationships that you will want to take extra care to develop over time and vet and nurture a little more closely than you do your other relationships.

This is your relationship with your banker and your freight factoring company.

BANK THE BANKER

You need to bank the banker as one of your first solid relationships. This is one of the most critically important relationships.

It's quite common for new freight brokers to need a line of credit issued to them. This line of credit enables them to be able to pay their drivers and carriers while they wait for the invoice to be paid by the shippers.

Not paying your truck drivers and carriers on time means they aren't likely to be quick to haul your freight in the future. Without carriers to transport your loads, you do not have a business.

Before you go into your local bank, you want to make sure you have your ducks in a row.

It's like walking up to a stranger and asking them to let you borrow $500.00 until payday on Friday.

You need to get to know your banker really well, and you will want to come with a detailed business plan. It helps if you have personal or even business accounts already established at the bank you want to work with for your brokerage firm.

They will already know you, and what type of customer you are. They can immediately gauge your trustworthiness based on your history with them.

Be sure you have drawn up a package that can clearly show to the banker and the bank that you are not a potential credit risk. They will also see a profit and benefit by working with you and offering you a line of credit.

FREIGHT FACTORING COMPANIES

Factoring companies (https://www.interstatecapital.com/factoring_industries/transportation-distribution/) are designed to help you as a freight broker improve your cash flow through a process called factoring.

This process allows you to double, and in some cases, triple the size, profit, and growth of your brokerage business even more.

Explanation of Factoring Companies

You agree to haul 10 loads of apples from a farm in Florida to a grocer that operates on the West coast. You are responsible for contacting the trucking company, and for this specific job, arranging the transport with a temperature-controlled fleet to keep the apples fresh on their journey.

The apples are delivered on August 1, but the farm in Florida operates on a 60-day payment term. They won't be paying you until October. Your carriers and drivers will not wait that long to get paid, nor should you want them to if you plan on keeping them on the road.

You will factor the invoice from the shipper/the farm, and send it to your desired factoring company to manage the paperwork and process at this point. They will verify the delivery date, the invoice from the shipper, the BOL, rates confirmed, and additional surcharges and fees, if applicable.

The factoring company then pays your driver/carrier for you from its own pool of funds. This procedure eliminates the need for you to process payments to your carriers from your own pocket.

Most factoring companies will cover up to 90% of your invoice via wire transfer or bank deposit within a few hours of the cargo being delivered.

Once your shipper has paid the invoice, the factoring company will wire you the remaining 10%, minus a small "factoring fee."

It is my advice that you use that advance to invest in new equipment or technology, pay outstanding bills, hire more sales reps or employees, or do whatever is necessary to increase your customer satisfaction and profitability.

What is Factoring?

Factoring is essentially a form of financing for the transportation and logistics industry. It's the perfect solution for the freight broker business model in particular.

Factoring is the process of paying for delivered goods, prior to invoices being settled. This allows you to get paid sooner than 30 or 60 days, so your carriers are not waiting to get paid.

The factoring company is technically buying your invoices to pay the motor carriers on your behalf, based on your instructions. They then turn around and collect the invoice from your shipper and pay you the rest of the invoice after their fee and carrier costs.

The Factoring Application Process

The application process is quick and painless and does not require that you have a good credit history or collateral in order to get approved for factoring.

This is not a loan and does not need to be secured by your personal assets. The factoring company uses your customer's credit and their ability to pay their invoices, not your credit, for determining the application approval. It's also much faster and less hassle than getting approved for a bank loan.

Without cash flow, it's hard for you to be able to invest in your business. Factoring is a non-traditional way of meeting those needs, without the stringent requirements.

Chapter IV: The Working from Home Mindset for Freight Brokerage Firm Owners

If you are accustomed to working in a corporate environment and commuting to work every day, adjusting to work at home life is going to prove to be a fun and exciting challenge.

Hopefully, the tips I share with you here in this chapter will help you to avoid the work from home blues, stay productive, and be laser-focused on your freight brokerage firm.

Maintaining Laser Focus and Getting Organized

How many times have you been working on something important and an email or a Facebook ding on your phone tears your attention away?

We've all been there, done that. I can't tell you how many times I've said I'm only going to get on Facebook for "a second," before I know it, a whole thirty minutes has passed!

While working from home, it is extremely easy to get distracted. Usually, we forego standard office rules.

For example, if you work in an office building, you may visit the breakroom twice a day. You probably go there once in the morning for your coffee, then at lunch to warm up your spaghetti-o's, maybe again towards the end of the day for a quick drink of water.

That's corporate America. Nobody would look at you differently if you went into the breakroom two to three times in an 8-hour shift. You probably wouldn't even think about doing it more often than that.

Why is it when we telecommute, or work from home, we are in the fridge or making pots of coffee every hour?

AVOIDING BAD WORK HABITS

How do you avoid adopting bad work-at-home habits from the start?

Treat your home office as if it were an actual office, with other individuals there.

You wouldn't get up in the middle of your shift and drive home to start a load of laundry or take a shower. Likewise, you shouldn't feel it is ok to do so in the middle of operating your busy work from home freight brokerage firm.

Truckers and shippers depend on you to be available and focused while relaying the right information when it's supposed to be sent.

Try taking a shower first thing in the morning. Eat a balanced meal. Put clothes on to go to your home office just as you would wear to a brick-and-mortar office. Clothes can change your entire mindset.

Another useful tool that I put into practice to help me stay laser focused was I specifically scheduled tasks into my calendar.

For example, if I wanted to take a lunch or walk the dog, I'd put it in my calendar as an appointment. I set a specific time of day to check social media, so I'm not stopping every time I hear a ding.

Get into your own rhythm and schedule your activities so you find the time to do them with discipline, and not sporadically.

TIPS FOR STAYING ORGANIZED

In addition to staying laser focused, you have to be equally organized, especially while operating a freight brokerage firm with so many details and papers involved in the process.

Do not get stuck in the trap of filing everything on your desk or in a pile in the corner.

If you have been spoiled by corporate office cleaners that make sure you have a spiffy keyboard each morning free of yesterday's lunch, then your first inclination might be to automatically forego doing this on your own for your own equipment.

Clean off your desk each night as your final act of the day. That way, when you start your day tomorrow, it's fresh and clean and reflects back to your mindset. There's something calming about walking into an office with a clean desk and a clear set of priorities.

This website has a HUGE list of free resources for working at home.

https://www.theworkathomewoman.com/free-resources-business/.

Working Alone: Your, Yourself, and You

Do you enjoy water cooler talk or listening to Rose from HR's puppy stories? If so, then working from home alone is going to be a challenge.

If on the other hand, even if you do not enjoy it, eventually you will want to have some kind of interaction with other people that you usually get when working in an office.

Who will you share your weekend date night stories with? What happens to the quiche lorraine in the breakroom every morning? What about the chance to eat lunch with your closest pals at work?

At home, there is literally no one with which to do those things. The more you are in confinement, the easier it becomes to forget how to be social.

By nature, we are born to be social butterflies. Even if you enjoy solitude over the company of others, you might not be aware of just how much we as human beings rely on external stimulation until you don't even realize that it is gone.

It is not healthy for us to spend too much time alone with our own thoughts. There are plenty of research studies that prove this point.

AVOIDING THE WORK-FROM-HOME BLUES

I have been working from home for 10 years, and I've come up with a system for avoiding the work at home blues. Feel free to use these tips to develop a routine of your own.

Plan your day the night before. Remember how I talked about being laser-focused and not getting distracted with things you can do at home? It's especially difficult for home-based business owners to keep their work and life balance separated.

There are endless possibilities for us to slack off all day, every day. There is nothing more important to your success, and the success of your business, than being able to have clarity and foresight into your day, planning what you want to get done.

When your feet hit the floor, become clear on your day's priorities. This way, you don't have any excuse for being distracted and not getting anything done. It is also a great way to train your brain to start thinking about your day in your sleep (https://avc.com/2011/06/subconscious-information-processing/). It's a method called subconscious information processing. You can learn more by clicking on the link to the website listed above.

Create an End of Day Routine. Just as you create a plan to start your day, you also need one to end your day, or you could end up burning out.

The flip side of the coin with distractions is, because you are working from home, you essentially don't have a reason to stop working and may let things go around you.

Find a way to wind down and begin to unplug yourself from professional work. It's not a conversation, but more of a routine.

Set daily reminders for yourself. Create the reminders for any small task or thing you want to do until it becomes a routine. Use Google Keep or Google Calendar on your mobile phone and computer to keep you on task.

Find time to socialize with others and actually leave the house once in a while. This is probably the most important thing about working alone. Take a walk, killing two birds with one stone by getting in some healthy cardio. Take your laptop to the park when the weather is nice, or go to the local coffee shop.

Join local meet-ups with others in your industry. I learned that by doing these things occasionally, I was more apt to follow my daily routine. I was looking forward to these outings as rewards throughout the week. Find a balance that will work best for you. You will reap the rewards in both your personal and professional life.

Now that you have an idea of the mindset, let's talk about a few skills you are going to need when working from home.

We will wrap up this chapter with your home office set-up. That's always fun, especially if you are starting out with a blank slate and room to be creative.

Developing Your Communication

I'm not going to insult your intelligence and pretend to teach you how to develop basic communication skills. You are a savvy business owner, and you know what it takes to communicate, or you wouldn't even be considering opening your own freight brokerage firm from home.

What I am specifically talking about here is communication skills and communication with your truckers and driving team.

As your freight brokerage grows, you are going to have truckers and drivers located in all areas of the United States. That often presents a challenge when trying to communicate with multiple drivers, on different schedules, time zones, and deliveries.

Luckily, there are a few tricks I learned along the way that can help you greatly increase the way you effectively communicate across your entire team.

It's important that you have an open-mind to modern technology, a dedication to follow through, and possibly make some in-house adjustments. Whatever the outcome, any combination or all of these things will help your business grow and scale.

"If you want to be able to compete with the big dogs, you have to learn to lift your leg" is a saying my grandfather always taught me. He was such a genius.

So let's talk about ways to improve communication before we have you shipping fleets of trucks across the country.

TALK THE TALK

I'm not talking about saying, "Breaker breaker one niner" when answering a call from one of your truckers. I'm referring to the words and terminology that you use when you speak to them.

There was a time when there were dispatchers for trucking companies, sitting in an office in an organized setting. They weren't the actual CEO handling the calls and making sure shipments got to where they needed to be or connected drivers, etc.

Back in the day, when a truck driver wanted to retire, he went to work in dispatch. He had the experience, he understood what it took to communicate with other drivers, and he was able to deal with situations and the responsibilities of his position.

Today, however, is a different story. Several factors make it easier for anyone to get into whatever field they choose. These factors are technology, an increase of women in the trucking industry, more home-based businesses, and online college training.

It can be hard for non-drivers to understand the life of a driver. A driver is on the road 24/7. They are therefore usually unable to empathize with the life of a home-based entrepreneur telling him where to pick up his shipments.

It's a paradigm shift. You or I will never know the frustrations, thank goodness, of having to find a parking space when there is no loading dock, or being 4 hours late on a shipment because of construction in the city that isn't clearly shown on GPS.

Just the same, they don't understand what it takes to cover when they are late, find replacement and coverage carriers, and communicate with angry shippers and clients.

It's important that you start with a clear empathy as to where they are coming from so you can show them how to treat you in return.

Both you and your drivers know that getting your load from one destination to the other is not a sleight-of-hand. There are any number of events going on at the same time, out of plain sight, in order to keep the wheels turning. The only way for anyone to have any success is for both parties to work together with proper and timely communication.

UTILIZE DIFFERENT TYPES OF COMMUNICATION

Always determine what type of communication is best for your team and its efficiency. Don't rely upon someone else's business model. A few ways to communicate include satellite communication, SMS messaging, email, phone, and even video chat.

There are some conversations that you need to have with your driver that are not appropriate to have via text or email. After a phone call, send an email to recap details.

Texting is a quick and reliable way to get a message out that is free to use. It is an urgent way to alert drivers to changes or road and traffic blocks.

Email is better for longer forms of communication, memos, and companywide announcements. Emails are also needed for confirmation and follow-up. Do not use email for urgent matters or sensitive, personnel issues.

Satellite is more for load tracking and provides a GPS tracking on your driver's location. It's great if you have lots of drivers on the road at one time.

The most important takeaway is to try to fully comprehend the stress related to driving and on-the-road living in addition to using the following techniques.

RESTATE YOUR VALUES AND BUSINESS IDEALS

Don't just talk about it, be about it!

Make sure everyone you hire to work with you knows your commitment to transparency and timely communication.

Make sure you emphasize that your dedication to clear, dependable communication is at the core of your values, and not just a cute little company slogan.

Be sure you are firm in requiring they uphold the same values. They must do face to face meetings, phone calls, emails, and text messages with each other on a consistent basis. If they cannot do that, then you do not want them on your team anyway.

Once they understand your commitment, then you need to arm them with the right tools to actually make all of this happen.

STAY TECHNOLOGY CURRENT

The people aspect of effective communication is easy. Finding the right platform to make that happen, however, requires a bit more effort at least initially in the selection phase.

There are tons of sites, packages, gurus, and products on the market, each offering a range of features to help you track your shipments, communicate with the drivers, and members of your team.

My top technology recommendations are:

- Copilot Live Truck is a GPS system using voice recognition.

- Uship Mobile is great for home-based businesses to receive automatic notices about bids.

- Trucker Tools provides coupons for your truckers to use at each of their stops.

- Trucker Path shows all truck stops, rest stops, parking, and weigh stations.

- Weather Underground keep truckers up-to-date with weather that could cause delays.

This list is by all means just the tip of the iceberg. Be sure to also look for communication tools that alert your drivers about construction, roadblocks, or traffic jams in real time.

BE CREATIVE

As I mentioned, you will want to incorporate video conferencing for the occasions when your truckers are out of range of cell service.

There are several options you can use. Skype and Google Hangouts are free. There are many other options if you can spend a little money to invest in more features.

Some video conferencing programs can even hold up to 250 people at a time, which may be necessary as you grow your business.

SHARE CONTACTS AND CREATE LISTS

With the more contacts you have, you will want to make it easier for your team to have access to them without always having to come through you to get them.

As you share contacts, share checklists for each contact and stop points for your drivers. Create a checklist they can print out and take with them on each load. The checklist is a set of reminders and important contacts they need while on their trip.

WORK ON YOURSELF TOO

Any true leader will not ask someone to do something that they themselves wouldn't do. This section is about you, as the owner of the company, setting the standard for the rest of the organization.

Take measures to improve your own communication skills.

You can do that by making sure you have clear, succinct, accurate, and consistent communication. For example, when communicating by email, be sure to not bury the important information in inconsequential rambling or personal questions.

Do not write anything angry or with extreme emotion; save that for a phone call.

Always command respect and not fear in your communication.

THE LAW OF RECIPROCITY

If you want your employees to take your direction, to let you lead, then you have to listen and respect them in return.

Make sure you take all of their suggestions and feedback seriously. Actually try to use this feedback to improve business operations and bring about change. By doing this, you let your team know that they matter, that you are indeed listening to their concerns and value their input in the business.

I hope by now you feel as if you can build a solid foundation for communicating effectively with your truckers and the rest of your team.

There are tons of free courses online that can help you build your management communication skills. Do your research and find one that you can easily take in your spare time. Start implementing the strategies you learn a little at a time for a larger and longer reward.

Let's take a look at how to set up your home office to help you stay productive and on task as we wrap up Chapter IV.

Setting up Your Home Office for Success

At the end of 2017, there were over 18,000 registered freight brokers in the United States. More than 40% of these freight brokerage firms are operated from a home office.

For some people, that means a corner in their bedroom, a kitchen counter, or a dedicated home office.

Setting up your home office to operate your freight brokerage is extremely easy to do. I'm going to share with you just what you need and how to do it, the right way.

CREATE YOUR SPACE

Regardless of where you decide to work, it's important that you have a dedicated space to do so and be comfortable there.

Make sure it is a space that can allow you to have access to everything you need within an arm's reach and not scattered all over the house.

Make sure where you have decided to set up your office has plenty of natural light. Natural light is a wonderful source of energy and can affect your mood and your work product.

If you have an outside view, that's even better. Just don't get too distracted daydreaming out the window.

Be sure your space has enough room for you to have storage cabinets and/or file drawers to stay organized. Having easy and instant access to your important documents and resources is critical to your daily routine.

TOOLS OF THE TRADE

There are a few necessary tools you are going to need to help you operate your business efficiently.

- Unlimited Phone Coverage. You are going to need at least one business line, possibly two if you want one line for your shippers, vendors and clients, and possibly a different one for your truckers. You can start with one line and grow to two or more as needed.
- Unlimited internet access with high-speed service. You can choose whichever provider in your area has the best deal, service, and quality.

- Computer with 2 Monitors. A fairly new computer with two 17-inch monitors to function as a dual screen. Be sure to go with a model that has enough storage and speed to handle your TMS software and any other tools you need to run during the day. You can find great computers at Amazon, Best Buy, or Staples.

- A quality email provider. You might want to invest in getting an official email to match your company name. That way you don't have to worry about Gmail, Yahoo, or AOL spam rules. You can require that all your truckers and staff get a Gmail account, if need be.

- A printer that also functions as a scanner and fax machine. They are often referred to as "all-in-one" printers. You can get one for relatively cheap on Amazon or at your local Walmart.

- TMS Software with a Load Board feature will save you from having to find a separate load board to track your loads, post loads, and search for available drivers and trucks in the area. A couple of the best on the market are Internet Truck Stop (https://truckstop.com/)

and TransCore 360 Express
(http://express.transcore.com).

- Any type of business software package like
  Microsoft Office for typing memos, creating
  invoices, and sending out important documents
  and files to your vendors and clients.

GET YOUR OFFICE FURNITURE

While I did say you could work from your kitchen
table, make it a point to budget and save for a
quality chair and work desk.

Keep in mind you will be in your office for 8 to12
hours a day. You need to be comfortable when
running your business or the temptation to get up
and go do other things becomes even greater. You
can go on Craigslist, find a local garage sale, or
check on the LetGo app for office furniture.

CREATE YOUR HOURS OF OPERATION AND NOTIFY EVERYONE

When you set your office hours, notify your friends
and family. This creates a consistent routine you can

depend on daily. It also allows you to avoid those distractions that come from unwanted calls and visitors.

Just because you do work from home, staying focused and having structure in your day will be the keys to your ultimate success.

I've been working from home for over 10 years, and in that time, I've learned that to be successful working from home. The bottom line comes down to your level of discipline.

In order to have a successful freight broker business and be a contending entrepreneur, you must eliminate outside influences that will steal your time and your business creativity. These cause you to lose focus.

I hope you have enough information to get your home office set up, and the mental capacity required to work from home. Now, it's time to look at how to price your freight brokerage services for maximum profit.

Chapter V: Pricing Your Freight Brokerage Services

Average Salary of Jobs Matching Your Search

Freight Broker **$185,000**

In USD as of Nov 17, 2016   90k   180k   270k

Average Freight Broker salaries for job postings nationwide are 221% higher than average salaries for all job postings nationwide.

National Salary Trend from Indeed.com
— Freight Broker

Courtesy of Indeed.com

The most important question you want answered is how much you can realistically make as the owner of a home-based freight brokerage firm.

Since our industry relies mainly on commission, there is no clear cut answer to that. The way to determine what you can make is based on industry standards and pricing models.

How Freight Brokers are Paid by Shippers

When you first start your freight brokerage firm, you are going to want to take extra precaution to read your shipper contracts. Try to stay away from the ones that expect the broker, you, to hold to a guaranteed amount of trucks with ultra-specific shipment times and locations.

This may be quite next to impossible to get done because you don't want to turn down business. What you can do to cope is to structure your pricing as "negotiable" instead of as suggested contract rates.

This is where you are going to want to let your master negotiating skills kick in. If you aren't a good negotiator, or don't have any interest in becoming one, then please, stop now. This is not the right industry for you.

You must be able and willing to negotiate your pricing, which I'll talk about in the next section, or your business is dead in the water.

EXAMPLE PAYMENT SCENARIOS

Don't panic! The calculation for pricing is fairly simple and will be simple for about 90% of your loads even as you become a seasoned freight broker. Let's look at some examples.

A shipper wants a load of household goods shipped from Atlanta to Ohio. The shipper may want you to accept a flat rate of $3,000 for the entire load. This is typical. Sometimes, shippers offer to pay you a rate per mile instead.

For the same trip from Atlanta to Ohio, a shipper may offer to pay you $2.00 per mile, and again, this is a pretty typical practice in the industry.

Another way that shippers offer to pay freight brokers is paying per piece that is in the load.

Let's say that the load from Atlanta to Ohio is oranges or strawberries. The shipper may offer to pay you $2.50 per bag of oranges, or maybe per crate of frozen strawberries, whatever the load is composed of.

Sometimes shippers pay by what is called "hundred weight" or CWT. That means they could pay a flat rate of $10.00 per hundred pounds.

Let's say that the oranges in this same example that are going from Atlanta to Ohio weight about 50,000 pounds. That means 500 x $10.00 = $5,000, not bad for a few hours of work.

One thing I want to point out is that you must be experienced in the requirements of each load and make sure you are using the best method of payment that allows you to see a profit and remain in compliance. Do not try to cut corners to make a buck. Major problems can arise down the line if you do.

In each of these payment scenarios, it's up to you, as the broker to determine your profit margin after you have paid your driver. On your shipper's invoice, you can most certainly include fuel surcharges, any additional stops that need to be made, rush accommodations, and more.

Keep in mind there are industry standards that will be included in your TMS software in order to take the guesswork out of pricing the services.

It's going to be up to you to work on getting prices down when you need them to be. Also, it's up to you to have a plan B in case your shipper is unwilling to negotiate with you.

The more you get experience negotiating rates, the better you will be. Let's talk about how you go about negotiating the rates with your truckload carriers so you can realize a maximum profit for you and your carriers.

Negotiate Pricing with Your Carriers and Truckers

Unless you establish rates with your carriers and truckers up front, each shipment or load will need to be negotiated. Keep in mind, as mentioned, there are plenty of rate calculators and tools available online. In most cases, you can find a TMS Software that offers that functionality as well.

You are going to want to find a reliable tool you can use to calculate rates because as supply and demand increases and the industry changes, so do rates. That means you will need to check current rates against the market constantly.

In 2017, shippers were paying $1.25 per mile on shipments going across the country from one coast to the other. For example, shipments going from California to New York.

By 2018, in some areas it was up to $2.50 per mile. When that happens, everyone is reaching for the same goal to move the shipment for as little as possible. Either that or they are recouping their costs in other areas like a fuel surcharge or using simple negotiation to get a better rate.

It is extremely critical that you learn about the rates and where your cargo is headed.

Shipments that leave from the New York and travel to California (east to west) are far cheaper than those leaving California and heading to New York (west to east).

The method is all determined by the actual products being shipped and from where. There is a much larger demand for shipments leaving from the west coast than there is the east coast. Therefore, prices go up.

Here are some sample costs for running a shipment. Keep in mind that these fluctuate with the market and demand.

Fuel Cost	0.60
Maintenance	0.25
Truck Payment	0.35
Driver Costs	0.35
Per mile total	1.55

As the broker, your truckers are going to heavily rely upon you to convey your rates to them.

Do your research on loads of similar products and distance so you can offer your drivers comparable rates.

Start at $1.55 per mile, that's the industry standard.

Often most drivers will accept that on top of a $100 fee. This is a completely normal practice for drivers.

Don't let $100 cost you thousands. To help you determine rates, check out the OOIDA cost per mile calculator below.

"The Owner-Operator Independent Drivers Association is the international trade association representing the interests of independent owner-operators and professional drivers on all issues that affect truckers." Check out their website on how to figure out cost per mile. (OOIDA)

https://www.ooida.com/EducationTools/Tools/costpermile.asp

The Importance of Doing Competitor Research

Once you know how to negotiate your rates, it is imperative to do some competitor research to make sure the rates you have chosen will allow you to remain competitive and relevant in today's ever-changing transportation industry.

Think of your competitors as anyone who can potentially offer the same service you do to your customers for any number of reasons. There are direct competitors and indirect competitors. Knowing how your competitors are positioning themselves will help you offer a better value.

DIRECT AND INDIRECT COMPETITORS

Your direct competition is going to be other home-based freight brokerage firms offering the same services, location pick up, drop offs, and products you ship, etc. The information you glean from your direct competitors is going to determine how you stand out from the crowd.

Indirect competition is going to be freight brokerage firms that possibly operate from a brick and mortar facility. They can also be home-based, but they offer services that you don't, or you offer services they don't. They fulfill the same needs in the industry that you do, but just in a different way.

Your indirect competition will consist of freight brokerage firms that offer their own equipment to move cargo. If you do not offer your own equipment, or if you do, they may not.

UNDERSTANDING POSITIONING

The same freight services can be offered in a variety of ways, situations, and methods.

The combination of these is what is known as "positioning." It is important that you understand what your indirect and direct competition's positioning is.

The more you can gather and analyze about your competitors and their positioning, the better you can set yourself apart to make your business more valuable. You become indispensable to your shippers, suppliers, and drivers.

It is ok if you and your competition have similarities in your positioning. The lesson is understanding how they position themselves and why it is effective or not.

This will help you to build and improve upon what is working, and make your positioning stronger in areas where it's not working for them. This also means knowing what they charge for their services as you determine your rates and negotiation rates.

UNDERSTANDING MARKET PRICING

You never want to charge much more than your competition. Conversely, you never want to underprice your value.

Knowing what your successful competitors are charging will help you to determine what price point people are willing to pay for your services. This is true for any business model.

The main thing you want to understand about pricing more than offering a cheaper price is being able to get and keep customers with a competitive offering.

Don't get caught up in trying to beat everyone that does what you do. It's quite impossible. Focus on serving your customers better with your competition research instead of beating the competition.

UNDERSTANDING STRENGTHS AND WEAKNESSES

Find out where your competitors shine, read their testimonials, see why their customers keep coming back to use their services. Is it something you can easily implement into your business? Can you offer something even better?

Keep your individualized offerings that make your business unique but also add those offerings that you know will help you get new customers and convince them to do business with you.

You are not going to be able to offer every single thing your competitors offer, especially just starting out. Don't focus on those areas you know you cannot improve upon or at least match equally.

It is not your goal to try and meet the industry's needs solely by yourself. If it were that easy, everyone would be starting a freight brokerage firm.

Spend as much time learning about where your competitors could improve as well. Discover your competitors' weaknesses.

Our strengths don't always seem like strengths to us. Why? Because they come naturally.

In identifying your competitors' strengths and weaknesses, you can begin to examine and determine your own. It can also give you an opportunity to see how your competition is meeting the gaps in the marketplace. This way, you can do better or even avoid the gaps entirely.

It is extremely important that you learn to negotiate fair prices. Study your competition and their positioning so you can better position yourself in a competitive and ever-changing market.

Equally important is determining what segment of the market you are going to serve, setting yourself up with the right tools, resources, and human capital, to maintain a healthy and sustainable business model.

Chapter VI: Choosing a Niche and Marketing Your Brokerage Firm

Have Your Ducks in a Row

Before we dive into the specifics of where and how to find customers, I think it's important that we start with the basics. Let's examine what any business should have sorted out before actually signing contracts and adding zeros to their bank account.

A business owner should know what his or her customers want to see from him or her before they even care about price.

Ensure your license is up to date and your bonds are kept renewed. There's nothing like trying to show people you are a serious business owner and not being properly licensed.

Shadiness is a turn-off in any business, and not being licensed is a red flag. You must make sure you have your Federal Motor Carrier Safety Administration licensure as we discussed in Chapters I and II.

Make sure that is the first thing you do before you even start marketing your services. There's no reason to rush on this important step.

The brokers who see the most profit are the ones who take the time to build the diversity of their trucking and cargo carriers. Not all cargo can be transported with an over-the-tractor-trailer (OTR) truck that you would typically see in front of a large department store unloading inventory.

This will also go back to your niche. If you want to focus on being an all-inclusive shipping solution for household goods, for example, then do that.

What I mean by all-inclusive, is that you ship by land, sea, or air, and you can offer flatbeds, trains, vans that are padded, or whatever. Decide that as you are choosing your niche.

Please be sure to vet the people you do business with, just as they are going to do to you.

Unfortunately, there are people in every single industry who choose to not abide by laws and regulations. That could include driving a truck without a proper CDL or even worse, without insurance.

Make sure you check and triple check your truckers and even shippers before entering into any type of contract. Look at your shippers for consistent and repeated complaints of non-payment in the past. That's a red flag.

Keep your business credit in good standing and keep your finances in order. A business that is going bankrupt won't attract new customers, and sometimes the desperation shows.

Just like you want to know your shippers pay their freight brokers, your shippers want to know that you too pay your vendors and truckers.

Pay all of your bills for your business down to a zero balance each month. Always pay it within the grace period. This is going to help you establish good business credit, and show your potential customers and truckers you are trustworthy to conduct business with.

Freight Broker Associations, Logistic Associations, Transportation Associations, The Small Business Administration, The Better Business Bureau, The TIA (Transportation Intermediaries Association), and other agencies are designed to help you live and die by the freight broker code of ethics. They ensure that everyone you do business with does, too.

Being a part of these associations show people you take your business reputation and standards very seriously. That's a great win for new clients. They love to see companies who can back up that claim.

Remember, at the end of the day, none of this will even matter if you aren't properly organized for running the freight broker business.

This means having your home office in order, gaining hands-on experience, and obtaining training. Most importantly, it means having an effective TMS software in place.

Finding a Niche

The freight broker industry is one that is full of fierce competition. It is important that you are flexible in the beginning stages of your business.

That doesn't mean you cannot identify a niche market to serve to help you stand apart from the pack. This will greatly increase your chances of running a highly profitable and sustainable freight brokerage firm from home.

Some of you may already have an idea of where you to focus your business efforts and marketing. This may be based purely on your previous working knowledge or just natural intuition.

Don't be alarmed if you don't already know. It is perfectly natural for you not to know yet, as you are just beginning your efforts.

THE IMPORTANCE OF FINDING THAT NICHE

The greatest benefit of becoming specific about who you will serve is twofold.

First, specializing in one area of the market allows you to create a level of expertise in one area. Working in that segment day after day will submerge you in every aspect of that particular sector of the industry. You will learn everything that makes it unique.

Eventually, your growing experience is going to help you and your freight brokerage firm to stand out as a leader and a trusted industry resource. You'll become a resource not only for your existing clients but new clients and vendor partners as well.

Second, you can focus your marketing budget, efforts, and message for one specific, much narrower segment. This increases your return on investment.

How to Find that Niche

Here are a few ways to help you determine your niche and stand apart from the competition while doing so.

Have you ever heard of UVP? It stands for "Unique Value Proposition." This is what makes your business unique from every other freight brokerage firm out there, home-based or otherwise.

Why should potential customers want to do business with your freight brokerage firm? Why not choose one that has been in business for years, operating with fleets of trucks?

Clear inspection of these differences and strengths will help you to discover the segment where your services can be of most benefit and have the most impact.

Evaluating Industry Segments

After you have identified your unique selling proposition, take some time to evaluate the industry segments one by one. Figure out which one is closest to your company's mission, vision, and service offerings.

Here is a list of a few segments of the industry you can examine further to determine your niche.

- **Local.** This is the easiest one to manage. Who is a better expert on the area where they live than you?

- **Cargo.** You can choose to only ship household goods or only produce. The choice is yours.

- **Trucks.** You may choose to only work with certain types of trucks. This may be trucks that help the environment, are good on fuel, or have other qualities you wish to promote.

- **Specialized.** You can choose to ship exotic or non-standard products for a larger profit.

Regardless of which area you choose, pick at least one and set about learning every single aspect of that segment, including the best ways of marketing to them.

We will discuss how to create a pitch that hits their pain points a little later in this chapter.

Be sure to seek out other freight brokerage firms who are specializing in the same niche as you and create alliances with them.

Make sure they are not your direct competition, but indirect, as we discussed earlier. Most of this can be found by doing what is called "market research."

Conducting Critical Market Research

In order to determine your niche, you need to immerse yourself and learn all that you can. That is called conducting market research, and it's critical for every new business.

Before you can create a strategy for the segment you chose and set out to establish yourself as an industry leader, you will need to prepare a few items. You will require hands-on experience, building your portfolio, and identifying market trends and insights.

Never underestimate the importance and effectiveness of thorough market research.

There are countless business owners, just like yourself, who started out by doing market research. Now they are enjoying a business that is able to remain competitive and stable.

This stability is achieved with constant research aimed at understanding their potential customers, identifying their customers' pain points, and remaining realistic about their competition and the competitions' positioning as it relates to their own.

Continual market research is the easiest way for you to be able to keep track of what is happening in the transportation and freight industry. You will be able to hold an advantage by continually evaluating your business.

Doing consistent, periodic market research should begin in your pre-launch phase and continually improve.

Having a better grasp on the marketplace from the very first day you open your doors will allow you to create a solid business blueprint.

There is no right or wrong way to conduct market research. It's an individualized process that is based on the company and its owner's goals and objectives.

What is it that you hope to learn or understand about the industry and the external influences on it? These intentions will also help guide your decisions on what to research.

Some of the most important questions of market research you will want to answer include:

- How effective are sales? Sales should be monitored on a consistent basis.

- What is the quality of service your competitors offer?

- What does your competition use to stay on top of communication?

- Who is the actual competition you face in the marketplace?

Once you have determined this information, you can search online for reports by your competition, examine their quarterly sales data, obtain surveys and studies, read reports in news outlets, and review data provided by the US Government.

HOW TO BEGIN CONDUCTING MARKET RESEARCH

So how do you go about starting market research? Follow these four steps in order to make your efforts successful.

Step 1: Before you spin your wheels looking for data and compiling reports, find out if someone has already done the work for you. Often a Google search will reveal market research already performed.

Step 2: Make sure the data you do find is applicable to you and meets your company's goals and objectives that you have established.

Step 3: Determine who will need the data and what they are to do with it once they have it. If it's only yourself who requires the information, you will make the determination for yourself about what to do with it.

Step 4: If you are using someone else's research, take the time to determine if you will still need to do your own primary research gathering. If so, who do you need information from?

UNDERSTANDING BUYER PERSONAS

As a newbie in the freight broker industry, as with any other industry, there are essentially three types of buyer personas. The research you conduct will enlighten you about how your low-hanging fruit and target audience are thinking while adapting to their core needs. This is what turns them from a shopper into a buyer.

The Savvy buyer is someone who isn't really too concerned with the caliber of the service or even how effective it is. They care more about getting the most bang for their buck.

A savvy buyer is always on the lookout for the best value. They monitor the prices of your toughest competitors. Your market research will help guide you on how to price your services accordingly and competitively.

If it turns out that your prices are not the cheapest in the industry, it is best for you to discover that before you start to market and attract customers. You should be able to fluently address what factors constitute the cost. For example, are you more reliable and easy to reach than your competition? Those are things you are going to want to answer right away.

The VIP Influencer is the industry leading expert with great influence. They are someone who is not just knowledgeable and highly skilled about the target market you serve, but they have an influence on the buyers and customers in their network. This is because of their credibility.

The industry experts aren't overly concerned with the cost of a service. They are more worried about the benefits and the superiority of the service or products. These experts can also prove to be an invaluable source and wealth of knowledge as you conduct your market research. Ask them for their opinions and about the market, overall. They have a lot of insight.

The Ultimate Customer is a buyer that actually consumes your services or products on a consistent basis, most likely daily. The ultimate customer is also referred to as an "end user," and they are also great sources for market research.

By talking directly with the shippers and drivers, you can better understand what they like and dislike about the current market. This information gives you an advantage over your competition as you produce a service that meets the needs and demands of the ones actually using the services.

OTHER WAYS TO OBTAIN INFORMATION

In addition to speaking to potential customers and online searches, there is a great significance in the market reports that are published quarterly online.

A quick trip to your local library can grant you access to these reports, as well as visiting business organizations and associations affiliated with the freight broker industry.

Be sure you look for the most recent published data that is applicable to your business. There's nothing worse than spending a lot of time finding information that is useless for making your business stronger.

Good research and a great pitch are what is going to drive your ultimate success as you start.

Creating a Pitch That Touches Their Pain Point

Before we take a look at some real-world examples, let's start by discussing what customer pain points are and why they are important to you as a new business owner.

DEFINING A PAIN POINT

A short explanation of a customer pain point is simply pain.

Discover what problem you and your services provide to help them eliminate or relieve that pain.

I'm not talking about a bad hip. That's not the type of pain point we are referring to here.

Customer pain points can be distinct, indiscriminate, and as diverse as your target audience themselves. Not all of them are going to be aware of what their individual pain points are. This can make your marketing efforts a bit hard to specifically target.

Your job is to not only show them that they have a pain point but guide them on what their pain point is and how your service can help to alleviate it.

TYPES OF PAIN POINTS

Be careful when just lumping customer pain points into "problems," as a general category. There are four types of pain points most buyers have.

- **Monetary:** This pain point is for the shippers who are paying too much money on their current shipments. They want to lower their costs but still receive the same quality service.

- **Production:** Are your shippers spending too much time getting loads and orders finalized? Are they looking to increase time efficiency? These are called production or productivity pain points.

- **Operation:** Do your shippers want to clean up their internal processes and operations? These are called operational or business process pain points.

- **Loyalty, Aid, or Support:** If your customers are not getting the support they need, or are not feeling very appreciated, then these are called loyalty pain points. They can also be called support pain points as well.

By determining your customers and clients' pain points using these categories as a guide, you offer your company and services as a major solution to their problems.

For example, if your shippers are struggling with a financial pain point, you can focus on how your services are lower priced than the competition. You can relate your pitch as to how they are going to increase their return on investment by doing business with you compared to what they are currently getting or would get if they went elsewhere.

Do lump all of your customers into the financial pain point and think you can win them over with only a lower price. It has to be a real pain point for them that you can actually solve.

Many of your customers and shippers are going to have compounded or even unclear pain points. It is for these reasons alone that you need to look at your customer's pain points as a comprehensive and personalized approach.

Present yourself as a solution to a number of their problems and not just one problem, or the most obvious pain point.

You now know what pain points your customer can suffer from. Let's talk about how you go about diagnosing what each client's pain points are.

DIAGNOSING PAIN POINTS

There are going to be instances when your customers are facing a coincidental pain point. Finding which pain point will be a motivating factor for change for you.

This requires you to do the research we discussed earlier. This research is a bit more detailed and individualized than the quantitative research we talked about earlier.

Even if you do have similar pain points, the reasons your customers are facing the same point could be as different as night and day.

Could finding the information be as easy as simply asking your clients and potential clients what they want and listening to what they have to say?

The answer is just as simple. Yes.

WAYS TO DISCOVER PAIN POINTS

There are plenty of creative ways to ask customers and potential customers what they want. You can host online focus groups whose goal is to go out and survey the customers. You can survey them yourself if you have built up your network from hands-on experience, as explained in Chapter I.

Do not simply rely on sales data alone. Your sales data doesn't intimately capture your buyer's pain points. This can often become your sales team's pain points over time.

Keep the two separate. Focus on what the "Ultimate Customer" persona wants in the end. That is who is buying your service.

MARKETING WITH PAIN POINTS IN MIND

Here is how you take the pain points listed earlier and market your services. We'll get into much more detail in the next section.

- **Monetary:** Remember, this is your opportunity to showcase a lower price than your competition, if it is indeed lower. Do not falsely advertise yourself. If you can help your customers improve their return on investment and then some, make sure you state it in a way that speaks to the niche market you have chosen to work with.

- **Production:** If you have taken the time to purchase an all-inclusive TMS software that allows your customers to have their own access to loads and shipments, showcase that to current shippers who are having a hard time communicating with their freight brokers. You can also start tracking how many times you are late on a load. Advertise that you have an excellent on-time delivery rate. Work on maintaining that excellent delivery rate by staying in constant communication with your shippers and truckers. Do not let the ball drop. Anticipate and scope out traffic, weather, construction areas, parking, and loading. These actions will help you keep a near perfect score.

- **Operation:** Every shipper wants the process of getting their cargo from one place to another as seamless as possible with minimal interactions. Highlight your commitment to communication, technology, and processes that you have that your competition may not have. Describe how that will help make their lives easier. "You call for a load, we do the heavy lifting" may make a great tagline to hit this pain point. (I should have thought of that when I got started. That's a golden nugget right there!)

- **Loyalty, Aid or Support**: Don't make the customer feel as if they are an intrusion to your day, just a meal ticket, or a means to an end. Find ways to include your prospective customers and make them feel a part of the process as they desire. Have enough consistent support for the things they don't wish to be included in. When you are marketing, use more words like you, your, us, and we, not I.

Proving that you can truly solve someone's problems can be challenging, especially when just starting out with no record to show for it.

USE WHAT YOU ALREADY HAVE

If you follow this guide and leave your hands-on experience with a solid Rolodex, you will have people that already know and trust you. Use those contacts as opportunities to grow and improve with people who can actually provide you with personal and professional feedback to see you improve.

Always grab customer testimonials and showcase those online in your marketing. This becomes validation for your social presence — that way, people don't just have to take your word for it.

You can always start with getting referrals from your hands-on experience and book of business you left with from your experience at the established firm.

Let them know you appreciate them for helping you get started. Offer them a grandfathered rate for a set number of years. This a way to show that loyalty we talked about.

Have fun in your marketing and remember to speak to the people who you identified as wanting to serve in the niche discovery phase.

Let's talk about where to find carriers and customers instead of just waiting on the phone to ring and hammering on your curated list of contacts.

Finding Carriers and Customers

Everyone starting out in the freight brokerage industry needs to have customers and a way to keep attracting new customers.

I cannot overstate the importance of technology's advancement in this industry with increased robust software. The same importance can be placed on the tried and true ways of finding customers that withstand the test of time.

The key is not to get a customer to send a shipment across the country with you just one time. You want to become a constant and dependable source of transportation for their cargo.

This will not cost more money or time if you choose to do it right the first time. You should not take shortcuts and use everything you have learned and implemented so far throughout this book.

One thing you want to avoid is going onto those organization message boards, or any online load boards to just simply pick through different shipments for the ideal one. This is the worst way to grow your business and attract new customers.

Load boards are extremely useful if you want an auction-style business. You would have to wake up each day and fight with people who have much more experience than you just to get a few crumbs.

I'm not saying you shouldn't focus on the clients you can get right now. As a newbie, you absolutely should. I just want to help you learn to secure long-term contracts that give you a sense of security while your business is growing and thriving.

ENGAGE WITH YOUR NETWORK

The quickest way you can find new customers is by engaging with your network. Either use the network you curated from your hands-on work or one you work to build yourself if you chose to do training instead of working at an established business first.

Learn how to work with other indirect competitors, as we discussed earlier to get referrals from them.

Remember, you are specializing in a niche. This niche is defined either by the type of products you ship, the locations you serve, or the types of transportation methods you have access to.

As you are doing your competitor research, locate those indirect competitors who are offering a service that you do not, and likewise, one that you do offer that they do not offer.

Ask them if they would like to be referral partners with you. Remember, it should be a win/win situation. It's not just about them helping you all the time. So if you have nothing to bring to the table, or don't plan on doing so, then you might not want to go that route.

USE YOUR PEOPLE SKILLS

If you keep in the back of your mind that shippers and clients of yours are no different than customers in a variety of other industries, you will have an easier time of speaking to your niche, marketing to them, and retaining them long-term.

Sounds pretty easy, right? I know, I do make it sound effortless, but it definitely does take some work and dedication for all of this to happen.

You will need negotiation skills, more than just an award-winning phone personality. You must actually be great at what you do. You have to become an expert with an extraordinary set of developed skills in the industry.

Be open and honest with your potential clients while you are just starting out. Use your individual knowledge that you have to stand out from everyone else.

Your industry knowledge is what is going to make or break you as a freight broker. Use any experience, and those of your competitors to learn and improve at all times.

Always let people know that you can be trusted, not just with words, but also through your actions. This includes the return on investment you promise and also solving any other pain points they have.

If you do not have shippers, you do not have a business. They are your customers at the end of the day. Your job is to connect them to the truckers in your network to move products around the country.

WHERE TO FIND SHIPPERS AND CUSTOMERS

So where can you find shippers hanging out in droves? What are they manufacturing? Where are they located or come from? How much cargo do they sell yearly? Those are the questions that will help you figure out where your niche targeted shippers are going to be, on and offline.

Remember my office story that prompted me to start my own freight broker business? Looking around your house can show you that just about everything on this planet is shipped and moved from one place to get to another.

Whether it is directly to your door or the store where you purchase it from, the majority of the American economy is transported by truck. This includes clothing, home furnishings, office furniture, food, livestock; you name it.

Do research to find out where your niche market is manufacturing the products you want to sell, then look at the associations to find credible shippers to match your customers' needs.

Sometimes, finding customers requires you to think outside the box.

When I first got started, I didn't have an awesome book like this to guide me. I took looking around my home a step further and looked at my box of receipts I kept for tax purposes. Once I had gone through those, I then logged online to Amazon and reviewed my pretty extensive order history there.

That's when I started to make a list. I based this list on my niche marketing. I found out where these products I wanted to ship were made and where were they being shipped to and from in the country.

Learn how companies are intertwined and connected to each other in the manufacturing and shipping process. Do not be discouraged if not every single lead works out the way you want it to.

The main thing is to keep at it and get back up on your horse. There is literally an endless supply of leads and possibilities if you look for them.

INVALUABLE MANUFACTURING COMPANY LISTS

As I was looking, I came across one of the most invaluable tools I could ever find. It's called "MacRae's Blue Book" (https://www.macraesbluebook.com/menu/product_heading.cfm?groupid=2533).

This website is a comprehensive yellow pages listing of detailed contact information about the manufacturing leaders and companies in the industry. You can do searches on products you want to ship. You will even be able to see what their rates are so you can make a solid comparison.

After you have done your comparisons, take a look at "The Industry Week 500" (https://truckerpath.com/uploads/2017/08/Top-500-Manufacturing-Companies-USA.pdf).

This is a comprehensive list of Fortune 500 companies that do a lot of business in the transportation and freight industry.

These companies, like IBM and Nike, Inc. have access to an infinite amount of resources when it comes to shipping and receiving freight. Start with this list as a way to help you begin locating suppliers for these major companies. Be their go-to person!

I was curious when I got started in the business about how many moving parts there were to one of those large 737 Boeing planes. Have you ever thought about that? That's a lot of parts to build a plane, right? There are over 367 thousand parts that go into making this beast of a bird. Think about it. The parts are not just in one convenient location. That many parts are coming from all over the world.

There are small, medium, and extremely large pieces of a plane. Likewise, there are small, medium, and large shipping businesses to handle all the different aspects of moving them.

Some companies are not able to meet the demands of shipping these parts, and that is where you identify the pain point and come in flapping your broker superhero cape!

Google all of the shippers that can meet the restraints of the parts, and there you have it. As a matter of fact, here's a search I already did for you, to save you some time. Suppliers of the Boeing 737 Airplane (http://www.airframer.com/aircraft_detail.html?model=B737).

This list includes contact information so based on your market research, competitor research, and niche/target audience, be sure to plug the ones you are going to work with into your TMS software. This way, you can keep them organized and easily available to contact.

If you are going to focus your niche on only shipping livestock or fresh produce, then you want to be sure to check out the USDA Farmers List (https://www.ams.usda.gov/services/business-listings).

There's nothing like eating a fresh strawberry in the middle of winter. Produce is a niche that ships all year round and in every corner of the country.

Produce and livestock are the highest in-demand cargo. Follow the same process for finding suppliers of airplanes as you would for livestock, but remember to focus on your niche specialty and don't try to be everything to everyone.

These are the best sources to start with. Remember that locating potential shipping customers is only a small fraction of what it takes to be successful in the freight broker industry, especially when operating from home.

You must take the time to network and build relationships with key players. Work on setting yourself apart with key positioning, generating respect, and gaining expertise to become an industry leader. You get what you put into this entire process, and it all starts with the knowledge and understanding of the moving parts.

Chapter VII: Regulatory Agencies and Resources for Your Business

Throughout the previous chapters, the different operating authorities and agencies have been sprinkled within the text. This chapter is designed to simply be a quick reference with links for you to access each of the resources, tools, and agencies you need in order to get started with your freight broker business.

Let's review the regulatory bodies and resources for your brokerage firm.

Links of Regulatory Agencies and Helpful Resources for Freight Brokerage Firms

"FMCSA"

https://www.fmcsa.dot.gov/registration/get-mc-number-authority-operate

"Department of Revenue"

https://www.aicpa.org/research/externallinks/taxesstatesdepartmentsofrevenue.html

"NTSB - National Transportation Safety Board"

https://www.ntsb.gov/Pages/default.aspx

"NHTSA - National Highway Safety Administration"

https://www.nhtsa.gov/

"Form BOC-3"

https://www.fmcsa.dot.gov/sites/fmcsa.dot.gov/files/docs/BOC-3%20Form%20508%20rev.pdf

"Small Business Development Center - SBDC"

https://americassbdc.org/

"Office of Entrepreneurial Development - USSBA"
(For SBA Loans)"

https://www.sba.gov/offices/headquarters/oed

"Alliance for Safe, Effective and Competitive Truck
Transportation (ASECTT)"

http://asectt.blogspot.com/

"Commercial Carrier Journal (CCJ)"

https://legaltechnews.tradepub.com/free/ccj/

"The Small Business in Transportation Coalition"

http://www.smalltransportation.org/

"American Society of Transportation & Logistics"

https://www.edumaritime.net/archived-
pages/american-society-of-transportation-
logistics

"Delta Nu Alpha," an international transportation

organization with a focus on education.

http://www.deltanualpha.org/

"Federal Highway Administration"

https://www.fhwa.dot.gov/

"National Industrial Transportation League"

http://www.nitl.org/

"National Association of Small Trucking Companies"

https://www.nastc.com/

"Surface Transportation Board"

https://www.stb.gov/stb/index.html

http://www.ltna.org/ a network of more than 200 local transportation organizations.

Transportation Intermediaries Association, an organization for North American transportation intermediaries, including property (freight) brokers, domestic freight forwarders, consolidators, ocean and air forwarders, intermodal marketing companies, perishable commodity brokers, logistics management firms, and motor carriers.

https://www.tianet.org/

Resources for Your Freight Brokerage Firm

Payment Solutions

https://cerasis.com/freight-payment/

Load Boards

https://truckerpath.com/truckloads/free-load-board/

TMS/Dispatch Software

https://www.softwareadvice.com/scm/transportation-management-software-comparison/

Document Imaging

https://www.microdea.com/document-management-software/brokers-and-3pl

Invoice Financing for Freight Brokers

https://www.ezinvoicefactoring.com/freight-broker-factoring

BOC-3 Process Agents - United States Corporation
Company

https://www.cscglobal.com/cscglobal/home/

Agents of Process Services

http://dotprocessagentsllc.com/

One disclaimer I want to add here is that I am not an
affiliate or paid in any shape or form by any of the
above companies. I mentioned them because I had
used their services before or heard good things
about them.

I strongly advise you to do further research and see
who else is out here and who may do a better job.

As you know, the world of the internet changes fast,
so what may be true or great today may not be so
great tomorrow.

Chapter VIII: Diversity and Growth Tips for Freight Brokerage Firms

Once your doors are open, it's best if you get into the mindset early that the only thing you can rely on being consistent is change.

If you want to be successful and remain in business, your first goal should be to embrace the diversity of the industry and all of its changes.

The word diversification tends to make new business owners and entrepreneurs a little trepid and green at the gills. Mainly because when you talk about diversifying your business, it means you must make some changes and evaluate current operations. By not doing so, you run the risk of losing valuable customers and vendors.

When done correctly and effectively, diversifying your freight broker business allows you to expand the outlook of the business, grow your bottom line, and start to specialize in other areas where you aren't currently serving a niche market.

This opens you up to a whole new pool of customers, and a wide range of services which you can now offer your existing customers.

When the time is right, never pass up on an opportunity to diversify your business. You'll know it's time to diversify because you will see a plateau of sorts in your profit.

Let's look at some ways you can grow your business through diversity.

Getting Customers

As a general rule of thumb, freight brokers should focus on having a single client that can account for at least 10% of their recurring business. It can be from a certain industry or a certain company.

Losing a client that size would be a huge loss for any freight broker firm.

Your goal should be to make at least 3 new contacts per day in hopes of obtaining them as a client. Make it a personal challenge each day.

While you are doing so, reflect on your indirect and direct competitors. This means utilizing all of the tools and resources they are using, including social media.

During my oppo research, LinkedIn was a huge lifesaver. They have search functionalities that allow you to perform targeted advanced searches to redefine your results and provide more accurate contact leads to potential clients.

Work on reaching out to your existing contacts from your networking and hands-on experience and ask them for referrals. Offer an incentive program to make it a win/win for everyone.

Add More Service Offerings

It's important that you go into this business with the mindset of growth right from the start. Your every business contact and action needs to work towards the evolution of your business.

Staying stagnant and continually repeating old habits is a recipe for disaster and invites possible threats that loom over you every single day.

To add more service offerings to your business and expand, consider expanding your niche or target audience. You could also simply expand the types of products you arrange shipping for. For example, you could add shipping wood, lumber, building materials, purified water, and even different types of produce or livestock to your repertoire.

If by some small chance, you are already niche specializing in these areas, you can instead look at other alternative modes of transportation. For example, if you are mainly using carriers that use flatbed trucks, you can expand into train, sea, and air transport as well.

The huge benefit to expanding your core services is that you will help to cancel out the seasonal downtimes and fluctuating market.

Take a look at the factoring companies available in your area and online. They can help you to obtain a credit rating and investigate the shippers in the industry. This will give you better insight as to when or if your brokerage firm is in a position to accept new customers.

Use Social Media Correctly

Social media is critical to your success and growth. Freight brokers who use social media correctly have an advantage. Social media provides invaluable tools to help narrow and define search criteria for a freight broker's low-hanging fruit.

Look to join and network in online groups where your ideal customers are hanging out.

Do not join a group of other freight brokers unless you are reaching out to form partnerships and referral networks. Other freight brokers are not your customers. While they may have industry knowledge you can glean from, they cannot lead to new business for you.

Try creating a blog. A blog can be a powerful platform for showcasing your knowledge, skills, promoting your business, and establishing yourself as an industry expert. Content is and always will be king, especially when marketing and promoting your business.

Distribute the content so it is actually consumed and read. Do not just post your content for the sake of posting.

Without thinking about its value and reach, you run the risk of alienating your potential customers by being self-serving all the time.

Interact in your groups on a regular basis. Provide feedback and thoughtful insight to the group members.

Respond to anyone who responds to you. It's called the law of reciprocity.

Don't just leave fluff comments or feedback. Your reactions, responses, and lack thereof speak to you as a business owner and to how credible you are.

Have a Plan B

As you learn to diversify your business, it's also wise to have a plan B. Remember, the only thing you can depend on remaining the same is change, especially in the freight broker industry.

While being at the forefront of embracing diversity and expanding your service offerings, you set yourself up for long-term viability in this market.

Being prepared for slow seasons and unexpected instability pockets will ensure you are never at the mercy of the industry's volatility.

As a freight broker, you need to be prepared to identify where you are weak and can be crippled. It can be in relation to weather where you live, technical issues, revenue, and financial matters.

Prioritize the risks that you face so you can devise a plan on how to get around that risk when it comes your way without crippling your operations.

Think of these questions as you create your plan.

1. What could possibly go wrong?

2. What are all the things that can happen?

3. How will you react to what happens?

4. How can you prepare in advance for risks and factors that could happen?

If you think that creating a diversification plan for growth and stability is something you can put off, imagine this scenario.

It's Monday morning, you walk in your home office, fire up your computer, and see an email from one of your biggest clients. They have sent you a 5-page email about switching to another freight brokerage firm, citing reasons that you could have prevented had you planned in advance.

Motivated? You should be.

Now get to grow your business!

Chapter IX: A Final Word

It's a cliché to say that all of our work ethics and preferences are diverse. That does not make this ideal any less factual.

The majority of American jobs force employees into a set work routine and format, which is ok for some but not for all. While some of us have always dreamed of working from home, it may not be an easy option.

What's exceptional about being a freight broker from home is that the option is yours and yours alone.

If you have a family, you get to spend more time with them by working from home. If on the other hand, you are single and like working around other people, then a shared office space might be ideal for you. You can be around people and still maintain your sanity.

Either option works fine. Try out some combination of the options available to determine what way is going to work best for you and your business.

Knowledge of the options you have about being able to control your work environment makes a big difference.

Being a work from home business owner, if you want to fire up the camper to go hunting or fishing, get yourself access to 4G Wi-Fi and go! You can work while camping in the middle of a scenic lake or under a sky full of lightning bugs.

But on the daily grind, make a habit of going into your work mode or space each day at the same time. What is most important is that you are able to distinguish what works best for you.

Most of us recall a time when technology professed to be the way to our freedom. Technology was a straight shot to leisure time and slacking off. It hasn't particularly happened the way we predicted.

In today's economy, technology more often than not tends to allow work and personal time to become indistinguishable from one another.

That does not have to be such a terrible thing.

When you become a freight broker, being accessible to your suppliers and carriers is an integral part of the business. While for some markets this high-tech imposition is a complication and a distraction, for freight brokers it makes achieving the essentials much easier.

At the same time, with the price of fundamental freight broker technology (think iPad, a Wi-Fi connection, and a smartphone) diminishing constantly, technology is making it easier for freight brokers year after year.

When this trend is combined with the plentitude of the various brokering software available in the market, it is extremely painless for freight brokers to embrace technology on their own terms.

For many of you, what's going to be the most attractive thing about being a freight broker is the freedom and independence that it affords.

Working alone day in and day out is generally terrifying. Fortunately, it's completely doable for you to be a fully independent broker from your home, but still get the help and advice you need when you encounter troubles. These issues can be anything from late payments, hard to understand software, legal jargon, or claims filed against you.

This is where it becomes critical to build a strong network of supporters with experts like your attorney, long-time shippers, and your surety bond issuer.

For your surety bond provider, make sure you find a credible and well-regulated agency with a positive record and attitude to match. Their experience and leadership will help you avoid making costly mistakes and claims if they should happen to you.

If you combine all these teachings in this book, it's going to be quite clear to you how freight brokers are able to maintain their success.

At the end of the day, the key is having the resiliency to seek out what works for you and stay the course.

There is no cookie-cutter template for a successful freight business and be leery of anyone trying to sell you one.

I wish you the best of luck in your future freight broker business.

Remember, Google is your best friend next to this book.

Happy brokering!

Chapter X: Glossary and FAQ for Freight Brokerage Firms

This chapter is a glossary of freight and transportation industry terms followed by a section of frequently asked questions.

A

Adjustments When a shipment is delivered. There may be times when an adjustment to the standard shipping rate applies. For instance, if there are any discrepancies in the original cargo quote from what is actually delivered. These adjustments can be anything from the weight, the type of class, and even the dimensions or location, in addition to performing any additional services that aren't a part of the load. Adjustments are things that can cause your invoice to be shortened. Do your research on how to avoid adjustments with your shipments.

Agent is the person responsible for acting on behalf of another company or individual, with limited or full authority to make businesses decisions. In the overseeing the procedures related to customs, documents, and even insurance. They shipping industry, an agent could be responsible for receive their payments as a portion of each transaction.

An Axle Load is the amount of weight the roadway feels, due to the total weight of any given axel. It is the total weight of a shipment that rests on any given axle.

B

Backhauls This is the industry term for when a shipment is on its way home after dropping off a load (its freight), but there is not an original order to pick up any cargo upon dropping off. The shipper will often offer you an incentive to ensure the delivery gets made. Often times, the trip will be back to where the original load was picked up.

Beneficial Owners are legally the rightful owners of certain property, even though the legal documents may have someone else's name on them. You will typically only see this term used in train and ocean loads.

Bill of Lading (BOL) are the legal contracts between all parties involved. These parties are the shipper, you as the freight broker, and the trucker or carrier. It details every single aspect of the shipment, including exactly what cargo is being sent and who is going to receive it.

Blockings & Bracings these are any type of support used during a shipment that keeps the products or containers securely in place during the trip. This is an industry-wide standard used by the best in the industry for the safety and security of their loads.

Blind Shipments These shipments are what the industry refers to anonymous shipments. This is where the shipper and the person receiving the shipment know nothing about each other. On the BOL, the shipping and receiving parties will be listed as the buyer instead.

Bogies This is a term used in the railway industry that relates to a type of enclosure with wheels where a large canister or container is placed for a cross-country trip.

Brokerage License is the legal binding document that you, as a freight broker, must obtain to be able to operate your business and make freight arrangements. There are different brokerage licenses for air and sea transport. If you plan on specializing in sea transports, you will need to get an NVOCC (Non-Vessel Operating Common Carrier) licensure. If you plan to specialize in shipments by air, you will need to get an IAC (Indirect Air Carrier) licensure from the IATA, International Air Transport Association.

Bulk Freights are types of shipments which do not require multiple containers inside the truck, nor does it contain a bunch of packages. Bulk freight typically comes in liquid or grain form.

C

Cartages This is a term used in the industry that refers to local shipments within the same area or the same city.

Chassis is an industry term related to trains or an enclosure on wheels. It can also indicate locks and more ways to secure the container for the shipment.

Classifications These designations are given to each shipment in order to determine the correct transportation shipping charges. Classifications only apply to cargo that is less than a complete truckload called an LTL (Less than Truckload).

Concealed Damages are damages not visible to the naked eye. It is only revealed when the packages or containers have been opened.

Consignees are the individuals who are responsible for receiving the shipment and are on the hook financially if something goes wrong.

Consignors are the people who are responsible for sending the goods to the consignees. They are legally the owner of the shipment until the consignee has accepted the item and paid for it in full.

Consolidated Shipments are ones in which there is more than one shipment combined together to save costs on freight. This is a common practice in LTL

(Less Than a Truckload) shipments and typically results in making several stops along the way.

Containers resemble tractor-trailer trucks without wheels or a cab. It is the most popular form of shipping goods in the United States and across the world. They all come in one standard size to ensure they can fit on any truck, train, or container ship.

Cubic Capacities The industry standard measurement is the cubic foot. Any truck, rail, or container ship is measured in cubic capacity. You will want to do your research to learn how to avoid any violations of this regulation. These violations typically occur when the shipment exceeds the size capacity of the vessel.

Customs Brokers are the licensed agents designated by the United States Treasury Department to regulate any and all freight imports and exports as it relates to United States Customs. The customs brokers are legally required to be used on any and all shipments originating from or going to Canada.

E

Embargo is an unfortunate incident that would ultimately prevent a shipment from being received or handled. In most cases, an embargo is the result of an international struggle or sanctions that have been imposed on certain goods, countries, or even groups of people. There are even rare occasions when an embargo can include natural disasters like floods and tornadoes.

Exceptions are problems, damages, and shortage or overage issues with a shipment when it's delivered. An exception will be noted on the BOL (Bill of Lading) and must be acknowledged before it is signed in order to identify there was a problem that requires an exception to the standard rates.

G

GVWR: Gross Vehicle Weight Rating refers to the entire weight of the vehicle doing the transporting minus the trailer weight.

I

Inbound Freight/Cargo is a major part of the day to day business operations of the freight brokerage industry. Inbound shipments and freight are those that come from various vendors across the country to use your services to ensure they have transport.

Interlines is the term that describes the transfer of a freight/cargo from one shipper or carrier to another in order to ensure that a shipment reaches its destination on time.

Intermodal Transportations are shipments that require more than one mode of transportation. They typically are from truck to train to truck again, but can also include transferring from truck to plane to truck again as well. Sometimes, the truck itself is a part of the shipment.

M

Motor Carriers are anyone who is transporting goods for payment.

Motor Property Brokers As a freight broker, it's your job to arrange to have shipments picked up and transported to a specific destination on behalf of an individual or business. The motor property broker, on the other hand, determines what each client needs, has tons of hands-on experience in the transportation industry with several contacts, and is exceptional at negotiating shipping fees and rates with each carrier. This is in order to meet everyone's needs with the client being the number one priority on that list.

N

Nesting is used to describe an LTL's (less-than-truckload) terms where the shipment is stacked on top of or inside each other. Nesting is a process that is designed to make LTLs a more efficient shipping process since they have less than a full load.

NOI (Not Otherwise Indicated) is the class assigned to a specific type of shipment that happens to be stacked on top of one another. This is similar to nesting, but the difference is there is no rate assigned or listed with the NOI. All freight ratings are based on handling, the liability of the products, the density of the shipment, and even the way the freight is stowed during transport.

T

Tariffs are the basis and foundation for establishing the costs and contract rates of shipment for all parties involved. The tariffs are on the products or goods being transported and not the truck, the carrier, or the shipper.

Through Rates describe the rates applied to the distances from the point of pick up to the point of drop off.

Time Critical Freight is the shipment delivery parameter set to the earliest pick up time as possible in order to accommodate irregular shipping and transportation requirements.

Time Definite Deliveries are deliveries that have a specific delivery timeframe. More often than not, it includes a specific time of day and on a specific date.

Transit Times are the entire delivery time from one point to the final destination of the shipment.

Truckloads (TLs) are the standard mode of transportation for most of the transportation and freight industry. They refer to trucks of average size (between 48 feet and 55 feet) in weight and in volume. There are trucks designed to be refrigerators and keep produce cool and dry goods dry.

V

Volume Rates are the LTL(less-than-truckload) freight terminology that refers to a minimum weight class of 7 thousand pounds or heavier. This is the same as 750 cubic feet.

W

Warehousing is how goods are stored at a warehouse and for how long. Shippers in the freight industry typically store their products until they are ready to be shipped out.

This list is by no means exhaustive of all the terminology related to operating a freight brokerage firm.

Google is a great and plentiful resource when it comes to finding different definitions and common terminology.

Chapter XI: FAQ for the Freight and Transportation Industry

Please use this standard freight broker frequently asked questions for quick answers to your questions.

We have covered these topics within the chapters, but this is a quick reference for you to use when you need to know the answer right away.

What does a freight broker do?

As a freight broker, it is your legal responsibility to broker property. This is the definition established by the Federal Motor Carrier Safety Administration (FMCSA), which is the regulatory division of the U.S. Department of Transportation (USDOT).

The freight broker is a licensed and registered individual or business that helps to ensure shipping of freight happens for various customers and clients.

What do I legally have to do to become a freight broker?

There are four legal requirements to becoming a freight broker and operating your freight brokerage firm from home or a brick and mortar facility.

1. Your broker's authority is provided by the FMCSA. The cost is typically $300 for each type of authority you want to have. You will need to complete an OP-1 form and file it with your authority application in order to legally operate your business.

2. You are going to need to obtain either a surety bond or a legally established trust fund. You can get one of these from your local bank or by doing research on top surety bond companies. The cost is going to be based on your credit score. As required by law, you must have a $75,000 valued bond or trust established. You will need to complete Form BMC-84 and/or BMC-85 to obtain your Bond.

3. You will need to hire a processing agent, by using from BOC-3, which typically costs around $50.00 per agent.

4. Finally, you need to get a UCR filing.

Is this really a lucrative business?

As of writing this book, there are approximately 15,000 licensed transportation brokers in the nation, but a large number are inactive. This is still a relatively new industry as there were only around 70 brokers in 1970.

It's estimated that freight brokers account for over 10% of the shipping industry or roughly $60 billion out of $600 billion in revenues. A recent article in the Wall Street Journal cited freight brokerage and logistics as the fastest growing sector of the transportation industry.

Can I become a freight broker without a surety bond?

You can open a freight agency or become a freight broker agent with little risk and without obtaining your own licensing. In that case, you'd operate as an agent under the umbrella of another broker's authority. You would do a split with the broker on your profits.

What equipment do I need to run a freight brokerage firm?

If you want to open a freight brokerage or agency, you'll need a computer with high-speed internet, a fax machine, a telephone, and phone service with inexpensive unlimited long distance.

Can I do this from home for the long haul?

Absolutely. Most agents and many brokers work out of their home office.

How long do I need to be in business before I see a profit?

It will take some time to build up your customer database, just as with any business that you start.

Typically it can take three to six months of disciplined work to show a substantial profit. Sometimes it takes much less time, sometimes more.

Once you begin securing customers, they normally have residual shipping, so the sale repeats itself over and over. Your level of success depends on many factors, such as your level of determination, your tenacity, and your genuine desire to help your customers succeed.

Where do I get customers?

In the previous chapters of this book, we go into detail on this subject. This book illustrates many different tools for locating your shippers, such as publications, reference sources, and internet sources.

Do I become a freight broker or freight agent?

There are many factors in making this decision, which we go over in detail during the course of the book. Three major factors are money, time, and experience. Either way, you'll need three to six months' worth of living expenses or a supplemental income while you establish your business.

Can I really make money as a freight broker?

As a full-time broker or agent, you can make anywhere from $40,000 in the first year to well over $150,000 after you have developed your client database. As time goes on and you continue to secure customers, your revenue will also grow. You set your own limits.

If I decide to be a freight broker agent, do I still need a license or bond?

You absolutely do not need to buy a license or a bond to be a freight broker agent. Working as a freight broker agent is similar in many ways to being a realtor, insurance agent, or hair stylist. The company you work under pays many of the costs needed to run the brokerage, so you don't have to pay them.

Others may convince you to spend thousands on a freight broker license and bond that you don't need as an agent.

Do I need to hire a lawyer to help me file my application?

No. The Federal Motor Carrier Administration's website has all the forms and instructions you need to file for motor carrier and/or property broker authority. They also accept questions by phone: 1-800-832-5660.

Can I hire an expert to expedite my application process?

No. The speed of the process is the same no matter who applies. You will be given a temporary MC number instantly. That MC number will become permanent and active after a 10-day waiting period once you have met the bond and BOC-3 requirements.

What is factoring?

With freight factoring, a factoring company gives a trucking company quick cash for accounts receivables. The broker is able to pay drivers and expenses in 24 hours.

The factoring company collects from your customer in the customary 30 days. This is an excellent way to stabilize working capital and boost your company's cash flow. This is not a bank type loan. This is an alternative to traditional bank lending and is especially important in the current economic climate. Factoring is an effective financing tool used by both small business and many Fortune 500 companies.

Made in the USA
Las Vegas, NV
25 November 2020